The Purse:
An Essential Guide to
Healthy Relationships

By

Montrella Cowan
MSW, LICSW

THE
Vision to Fruition
GROUP
PUBLISHING | INVESTING | CONSULTING | ACADEMY

The Purse

Copyright © 2020 by Montrella Cowan, MSW, LICSW

All scripture quotations are public domain courtesy of Bible Gateway: www.biblegateway.com.

ISBN: 978-1-7339413-8-9
LCCN: 2020908780

Cover Photo by Isaiah Mays

Format and Layout by LCB Consulting and Design

The Vision to Fruition Publishing House
www.vision-fruition.com

Dedication

Veronica Ross (March 13, 1954 - February 10, 2018)

To Mommy, who taught me what it really means to BE, DO and HAVE as a true Pisces.

*Mom,

While the world needs doctors, preachers, lawyers, reporters, bankers, and social workers, it could not function without people like you—hallmarkers and trailblazers.

Veronica, your *hallmark was a mixture of your shining silver hair and gold-plated heart, certified with the platinum qualities of unconditional love, loyalty, and joy.*

The smallest things would cause a smile to curl your lips and a twinkle in your eyes.

True Brooklyn Queen, that's who you were! Born, bred, and now expired here, we're just waiting for your face on the postage stamp to come in the mail any day.

Quiet as it was kept, without your glasses, Veronica, everyone knew that you were as blind as a bat. Beautiful being who was truly built like an Amazon, one of your personal songs could have been "She's a brick house!" Just as the Commodores said in 1977 when you birthed your second child. You with your hourglass shape that you passed along the way to your children and grandchildren like Miasia, for heaven's sake.

We cannot forget how at the tender age of sixteen, you gave birth to Rudolph, and not Santa's red-nosed reindeer. Yet, defeating all odds, you still walked across that stage among the top students of your Prospect Heights class. Next, you had the audacity to have three daughters? Montrella the social worker, Angelica the protective mother, and Sabrina the soldier.

Veronica, you were most proud of your four children, but remember they are only a reflection of your personal inspiration and amazing transformation.

When you chose to depart, it was on your own terms, in the comfort of your own home, a haven for many wandering souls, yet a placed filled with your heart.

How would we know this?

Because your last meal was fried chicken and chocolate cake, and we shall not forget the half-bottle of hot sauce with which you ate. And even though we cannot do anything but respect the way you checked out we will always miss you no matter what.

Though you never learned how to drive a car or really work your cell phone, don't worry, Veronica. Your great legacy of love, compassion, and wisdom that you created will be carried on.

Veronica, your beautiful spirit will always be with us!

---

*I read my poem at Mommy's funeral in Brooklyn, NY, on February 20, 2018, at Solid Rock Baptist Church.

Acknowledgments

First and foremost, I give the highest praise and thanks to God Almighty! Thank you, Father God for making me in your image and then giving me the testimonies to live through to be reminded of that fact. I thank my birth parents, Veronica Ross and John Henry Cowan. You both were perfect regardless of all your imperfections. Thank you for coming together and creating a love child—yours truly. I am so grateful to the two of you for every breath I get to take on this planet. I am made up of the best parts of both of you. I thank my two children. China Mo-Nay Cowan, thank you for forcing me to grow up and to keep growing. I am so proud of you as a person and all that you accomplished during your 25 years on this earth, especially my granddaughter, Sekai. May your soul rest in harmony and peace, China. To my son, Satcher An Kham Nu, a.k.a. Brother Nu, thank you for always putting up with me and believing in me at the same time, as a mom, as a person, and as an author, especially on this book-writing journey. Brother Nu, you continue to make me up my game in life.

I thank all my family members. You are women, men, and children with that "Empire State of Mind." You each are an inspiration to me in unique ways. I have to give a special shout out to my aunt Cynthia Hodge. Auntie, you are the best prayer warrior I have ever known. Thank you for being a constant reminder to me to keep my faith, especially in the midst of a storm. I want to thank my godchildren. Out of the many roles I play, being a godmother is among the most honorable and humbling. I am proud of you both TyJayee and Donte.

Thank you to my two BFFs, Ebony Johnson and Tyrona Bethea. You both are a daily reminder of unconditional love. Thank you for this love that has provided me with oxygen during my heartbreaking experiences and most highlighted experiences and everything in between.

I thank my pastor, John Jenkins and First Lady Trina Jenkins of First Baptist Church of Glenarden (FBCG), and the College Ministry in Prince George's County Maryland for ALWAYS reminding me to be who I am unapologetically, and more importantly, to fulfill my purpose on this planet. I also thank the members of the Founding Church in Washington, DC. You will forever have a place in my mind and spirit. Thank you, Reverend Willie F. Wilson, and the members of Union Temple Baptist Church for being like family when I felt so alone after moving from New York to Washington, DC. Know that I still remember and quote you. Thank you to Howard University School of Social Work!! Without each of you I would not have the tools to be as effective as I am as a social worker!

Last, but certainly not least, I want to thank all my clients. Nothing makes my heart gladder than to be able to hold up the mirror to you, help you overcome your personal traumas, and step into your greatness! You allow me to do the kind of work that does not feel like work at all.

Table of Contents

Foreword

Trauma.

It can be a whisper on the wind or a clap of thunder on a rainy night. It crawls past even the most secure defenses and makes itself at home in the bones of kings and poor men alike. I know the taste of it like I know the sound and shape of my own name. Hell, it's as much a part of me as my name, though for very different reasons. Once, it would have defined me. Once, it tried to define me. I had to teach myself how not to let it, and once I pulled its claws from my skin I sat down and set my mind to teaching others just like me.

Did you know that it is a noun?

A strange concept to consider — that trauma can be a person, a place, or a thing. That it's not just a word used to describe a being, but a state of being itself. It's defined by Webster's dictionary as:

> **a**: an injury (such as a wound) to living tissue caused by an extrinsic agent
> **b**: a disordered psychic or behavioral state resulting from severe mental or emotional stress or physical injury
> **c**: an emotional upset

Greek for "wound" or "defeat," I could write a book on all the ways it has made its presence known in my life. From being a little girl and watching addiction ravage my mother, to losing those I believed to be the loves of my life as a grown woman. It's an experience that leaves lasting psychological and emotional scars. It's trial by fire, a crucible of lessons learned, and for some a constant companion. No one escapes the touch of trauma in this life.

No one.

But if you're lucky, if you walk tall in love and faith, a precious few learn how to heal from it, learn how to transform themselves from chunks of coal to diamonds beneath the same weight that would have otherwise ground them down to nothing. Not only did I heal, I took what I learned and taught it to others. Happiness isn't a default. It's something you must work at, something you must fight for. When it comes to finding a healthy relationship after trauma has passed through like a tornado, happiness can feel like a bartering chip. Something you give away as currency or as a sacrifice so long as the person you are with doesn't hurt you as badly as the one who came before him.

I've seen it all before and lived through most of it at least twice.

Over the course of this book I hope to take you on a journey and gift you with the tools that I wished I had at the start of my own. Tools that I know better than to ever leave home without again. The idea of the purse as a teaching and coping mechanism regarding relationships after trauma has been on my mind for several years now. So many of the items that I carry with me on a day-to-day basis remind me of those lessons and tools that helped me reinvent myself so long ago. During the next few chapters, we'll be delving into several concepts. Some lessons will be preceded by personal accounts, while others will not. This is as much to walk you through how I came to find my own answers as it is to highlight the winding journey your path may take. Together, we'll figure out who you are and what you're doing to contribute to your own unhappiness so that we can then determine what it is that you can have once you've stepped out of hurt and into healing.

Some of these items may strike a chord, while others you're fine without. While we won't delve into every possible item, I will go over the ones I consider the most essential. For instance, some women carry around coupons and you'll notice that these aren't something that's mentioned. Not because they don't belong in a woman's purse—they have indeed earned their rightful place there—especially with respect to reducing the household budget. However, I chose not to go into detail about the part they play in relationships, because we don't want to "sell out" when it comes to the people we care about the most. Those we love deserve more than 50% of our love, effort, and time. You won't find mention of makeup, because we are not pretending here. The advice I offer is all about authenticity both with yourself and with your partner. If you want an inauthentic relationship, there is no need to read this book. Just keep acting and see how many clowns you attract. Lastly, since this book is more about overcoming trauma and personal hang-ups, we won't be discussing items like bobby pins either. They hold things in place when everything is already going well. You lose a few only to make the ones that remain take up more of the load to keep everything together—at least until you can buy a new pack to replace what was lost. Either way, bobby pins are for *after* you've put in the work, not before.

These pages, they focus on the before.

By the time we are through, you should be able to:

1. Address personal traumas.

2. Be accountable for your actions and choices rather than placing the blame on someone else (i.e., your parents).

3. Acknowledge the part you play in the cycle of abuse so that you can finally stop it.

4. Realize that everything is seasonal.

5. Find your inner confidence.

6.   Value all your relationships, even the crappy ones, for the lessons they have taught you.

7. Validate others and — most importantly — yourself.

8. Accept people for who they are and what they bring to the table.

9. Stop lying to yourself.

10. Develop healthy coping mechanisms.

Some of these lessons will be harder to learn than others, and that's OK. This book is a blueprint, a guide and compass to lifestyle changes and personal discovery. None of which ever happen overnight. The number one takeaway to be found here is that a healthy relationship is possible despite any personal trauma you've experienced. What I love most about my life today is that I get to help my clients ditch the unhealthy habits they've developed in the interest of self-preservation, so that they can have the relationships that they truly desire. Relationships that they thought were impossible.

I'm here to tell you that you are not broken. You are just as worthy of love as anyone else. But keep in mind that like anything worthwhile, healing is a process. This isn't a cookbook. I can't give you a recipe for self-love complete with ingredient list and serving size. I mean, I *could*, but even then, all the tips and tricks in the world are sometimes no match for good old-fashioned counseling.

Whether you need individual or couples counseling, the benefits of working through your problems with a trained professional are unmatched. It's true that going to therapy or seeing a "shrink" has a stigma—especially within certain communities. I'll admit that the media hasn't exactly depicted therapists in the best light but reaching out for assistance is one of the healthiest things you can do for yourself and your relationship. Because I focus on personal trauma, I help you *finally* let go of your past so that you can be in the present with your loved ones. It's the only way that you can create a healthy, whole, and fulfilling relationship with your partner, and *The Purse* was written with that exact goal in mind.

Regardless of where you are in your healing—whether you're testing the waters or have been struggling to make progress for years—I hope that this book can offer you a glimpse into what a session with me is like. I hope that you take what you learn and apply those lessons to your everyday life. I hope you read the affirmations scattered throughout these chapters and take them as the sign you may have been looking for all along. A sign that change is afoot. A sign that things can be better.

Lastly, I hope that the stories I share touch your heart and that just like the items in your actual purse, the fire that they alight within you, the desire for more, for better, is something that you never leave home without.

With Affinity & Harmony,

Montrella Cowan, MSW, LICSW, a.k.a Shernetter

~ Healing is a process. Let us begin now. ~

Introduction

There comes a time in every woman's life when she must brush away the cobwebs of who she used to be and step unapologetically into her true beingness. For you, that day is here and now. The house isn't as neat as you'd like it to be, but you and your date are going out to dinner, so it'll suffice. He'll never see the clothes tossed haphazardly towards the laundry basket or the dishes in the sink. He called a few minutes ago to say that he's running late, and normally you'd be upset, but this gives you time to do something you've meant to do for a while. You haven't been out with anyone for a long time, and you bought a new dress to commemorate the occasion. The small black purse you pulled from the back of your closet goes well with your outfit. Of course, it does. It's the purse that goes with everything—the one that you wear when you need that extra boost of confidence, the one big enough for your lipstick and a copy of the latest book you are reading. You bought it one day with your first good paycheck. It was more than you usually spend, but it was beautiful, so you figured, "Why not?" You told yourself that you deserved something nice, and now it's your constant companion when you want to make a good impression on job interviews and first dates.

But it's been months, maybe longer, since you cleaned it out and, now that you are already dressed with some time on your hands, you perch on the edge of the couch and decide to do just that. You unzip the purse and, at first glance, the contents within look overwhelming. No wonder you can never find anything you're looking for. You upend the purse on the surface of the coffee table, and the contents spill forth, covering the table from one end to the other. In your mind, you're already deciding how you'll divide it all. There will be three categories: items you use every day, items you'll only use in the event of an emergency, and things you'll probably need in the future. Technically, there are four categories if you count the trash.

You don't.

There's a hodgepodge of items to choose from, and you hesitate. Then, a leopard-print compact catches your eye. You reach for it, turning it this way and that and as if by instinct, you open it. Inside is, of course, a mirror. You meet your reflection's gaze. For a moment, the light from the lamp in the corner of the room bounces off the glass and into your eyes, and in that breath, you lose focus and your surroundings fade...

PART ONE: TO BE

> By three methods we may learn wisdom: First, by
> reflection, which is noblest; second, by imitation,
> which is easiest; and third by experience, which is the
> bitterest.
> —Confucius

~ *Be Love!* ~

Chapter 1: *The Birth*

"Calm down, Montrella."

The lights in the hospital room were blinding, and the nurse's voice grated on my nerves like nails on a chalkboard. I gritted my teeth, bearing down in a way that only instinct could account for. I'd been told not to push yet, but I couldn't help it. I wondered if this was what my mother went through when she gave birth to me. I wondered if bringing new life into the world meant breaking myself in half. Mostly? I wondered how I'd gotten to this moment in the first place.

I didn't know it at the time, but by all accounts, I was a statistic. One in every five women and one in every seventy-one men will be raped at some point in their lives. When you look at the bare bones, the reality of the world that we live in, it's enough to make your blood run cold. Out of that number one in every four girls and one in every six boys will be victimized before they turn eighteen. 12.3% of women and 27.8% of men are under the age of ten when their first assault takes place. Meanwhile, 30% of women are between the ages of eleven and seventeen when they're raped for the first time.[1]

I was a member of that 30%, though to the judging eyes taking stock of my situation I was just another "hot-ass", knocked-up teen. In the early nineties there were plenty of girls who found

---

[1] Available at: https://www.nsvrc.org/statistics as of 5/2020.

themselves in my situation. That part of the decade saw a spike in underage pregnancies and to this day holds the record at 61.8. While the rate of teen pregnancy has decreased over the last several years, the United States still has more reported teen pregnancies than in many other developed countries. I knew what people saw in me because it was what they saw in every pregnant black girl my age. Just by looking at me they assumed that I was the type of girl who ran wild and couldn't keep her legs closed. The details of my predicament meant nothing against the sheer stubbornness of their censure.

One of the first lessons I ever learned was that you can't please everybody. There would always be someone with something to say, some judgment to make, some assumption to make right. In a perfect world, I wouldn't have felt the need to explain myself or my baby, but that's not the sort of world that I lived in. Instead, everywhere I turned I had to fight back the urge to tell my story in its entirety. To explain all the nuances and pain that led to the swelling of my belly in the first place.

In my imagination, the older woman staring at me in line at the grocery store, the kids whispering behind my back at school, or the man on the sidewalk glancing over surreptitiously as he walked his dog would all pause and lend a sympathetic ear. In this fantasy, I'm brave enough to speak, to tell them about all the secrets I've been cultivating so carefully and reveal all the fears that have left me paralyzed over the course of those nine months. In my fantasy, I tell my story and—just as importantly–they linger long enough to listen to it.

That was one of the hardest things. Not telling the truth but finding someone with the compassion to listen.

In the end, the fantasy was simply that.

I never confronted those strangers and their silent—and often-times all too verbal—censure. The words remained stuck in my throat and I learned what I needed to at the time. Something that seemed all but impossible once I realized exactly what was in store for me. I learned how to push through. How to keep my head up regardless of doubts weighing me down. I learned that there was more to me, even back then, than what people saw.

~ *Remember who you are.* ~

Chapter 2: *Reggie*

If someone told me ten months ago that I would be giving birth to my first child, I would have laughed in their face. I wasn't the kind of girl that got knocked up. In fact, I had secretly made a pact with God that I wouldn't even have sex until I was married. I was proud of that covenant too. As it turned out, however, both 1992 and 1993 were full of surprises, and my life didn't seem at all to be going according to the *divine plan*.

Kirk Franklin sang once that blessings could be found in storms. Ironically, it is during the storm when one's vision is usually blurred. Not that I can complain. After all, diamonds are forged under pressure, and I'd experienced my fair share long before moving to Washington, DC, to live with my father and his new family. Back in Brooklyn, I'd grown used to making do and getting by; when poverty is all you know you learn how to do both with aplomb. But it wasn't lacking food in the refrigerator, being forced to eat those chocking thick welfare cheese sandwiches, or the cable getting turned off that eventually forced my father to ride in like a knight in shining armor to save me.

You see, my mother was a lover. It did not help that she was an attraction magnet with her hourglass shape, book smarts, generous personality, and bright smile. Like bees to honey, mom attracted men from all walks of life. The low-life guys especially were drawn to her. Still, she gave her all to everything that she did. No half measures. Which wasn't always a good thing.

Growing up, my mom often lost herself in the embrace of men and the good times she had with them. Following the many gifts that these men showered upon her, one very charismatic fellow, whose name ironically also happened to be Reggie, introduced her to drugs. He wouldn't do so until much later, after furnishing my mom's place with luxuries such as a brand, new washing machine and dryer. Such things were no small matters in the eighties.

At the time, my brother, who my mom had when she was sixteen years old, was out running the streets and gangbanging. This, coupled with the fact that I was the oldest girl, made me the next in line. That said, I was the one tasked with the heavy burden of holding the scraps and pieces of what we considered our family together and protecting my two younger sisters. It was a lot of weight for my thin shoulders. I felt especially responsible for my two younger sisters, and I worked hard to create the illusion that they were cared for and loved rather than having them see that we were really neglected and abandoned. Most girls look to their mothers for guidance and strength, but I found those things in the church. Faith in a higher power taught me what she couldn't, and by the time my biological father brought me to DC, it was the one constant in my life.

My father was a strict, no-nonsense kind of man from North Carolina while my mother was a vivacious, book-loving extrovert born in Brooklyn. How did they meet? It was the seventies and, even though my father was already involved with the woman who would one day be my stepmother, he was justifiably distracted by my mother. Distracted by her smile and the sway of her hips. By the way she would get lost in her favorite book or the boisterous sound of her laughter. Mom had this alluring, down-to-earth richness of soul that drew men to her like a lodestone. I am not sure what enticed the two of them more: the fact that my mother would stroll right through his girlfriend's house while she hosted card games, or that he would drop his girlfriend off first and my mom off last. Whatever it was, she and my mother were pregnant at the same time with my half brother and me respectively. Even I was surprised when my mom told me that she and my dad planned for me. Notwithstanding, a few years after I was born, crack hit the streets of Brooklyn and my mother began to spiral.

But we'll get into that a little later.

Regardless of what brought my parents together in the first place, my stepmother was the opposite of the woman who had given birth to me in nearly every way. For one, my stepmother didn't appreciate being saddled with me when she already had four children of her own to contend with. Not only was I another mouth to feed, but I was also a constant reminder of my father's infidelity.

While going to live with my dad probably saved me from a life of addiction and crime, not everyone wanted me around. When my stepmother wasn't being petty and spiteful, her kids were making sure I knew exactly what they thought of me. My stepsiblings looked at my faith as something to laugh at, and my half-brother was no ally. We were only ten months apart, which meant that our mothers' pregnancies had overlapped. His mom's prejudice towards me seemed to rub off on him though there was no excuse for the way he ridiculed me about my looks and found every excuse to drag me down. Hungry for companionship and a sense of normalcy, my family's emotional distance left me adrift in a sea of doubt and loneliness. I wanted approval, acceptance, something to prove that I belonged. Since I couldn't find what I was looking for at home, I searched for it elsewhere.

For a girl from Brooklyn who prided herself on her ability to adapt and thrive under pressure, I felt uncharacteristically out of my depth in DC. I would be starting high school soon, and I was painfully awkward and insecure. My faith made people think that I was either a prude or a snitch. Beyond that, I was too much of a nerd to connect with the other kids my age long enough to dissuade them of this belief. It was as if I was out of place in every corner of my life and I was continually trying to make up for some lack within myself that I didn't even fully understand.

In the end, I was determined to make a new start for myself. I'd left my mother's toxic habits back in New York, and this was my chance to be an average teenager. To do all of the things I'd once shied away from for fear of falling down the same slope that had tripped her up so long ago.

I wasn't my mother, I reasoned.

I could handle a little teenage rebellion here and there without getting caught up.

What's that saying?

"The best-laid plans of mice and men often go awry."[2]

That's what happened to me. Things went awry.

My first year in DC, I was lucky enough to find a best friend in a girl named Jade. We were around the same age, and I loved how bold and self-assured she was. Jade wasn't afraid of anything or anyone and being friends with her pushed me to step outside of my comfort zone.

One day, we decided to combat the heat with a trip to the local community pool. It seemed like every girl except me was in a two-piece. Like many girls my age, I wasn't as comfortable with my

---

[2] From Robert Burns' poem *To a Mouse*, 1786. It tells of how he, while ploughing a field, upturned a mouse's nest. Available at: phrases.org.uk/meanings/the-best-laid schemes-of-mice-and-men.html.

body as I could have been. My brother was always telling me my big lips, dark skin, and big feet were ugly. That they were something I should be ashamed of. I wasn't a fan of makeup either and he got on my case about that too, especially since I suffered from constant outbreaks of acne. All the judgment I got at home about my appearance convinced me that there must be something wrong with me. It didn't help that people nicknamed me "String Bean," "Skinny Minny," and "Bag-of-Bones." I was thin, and if it wasn't for my breasts, I would have been considered a rail. As a result, showing that much skin left me uncomfortable, and every causal glance aimed my way was foreign and unwelcomed. All I could think of was what my dad would say if he knew I was running around half dressed in front of all these grown men.

If I was honest, however, there was a small part of me that reveled in the attention. I was stepping into my womanhood, discovering what it meant to be a sexual being with an agency over my body, and I knew that those looks meant something. Something I couldn't put words to but understood deep down. It was an ancient, primordial kind of knowledge. Besides all of that, the thrill of doing something I shouldn't made my father's fictional disapproval worth the risk. It was the first time I'd ever done something remotely normal, and I wasn't going to back down because I was little uncomfortable in my own skin.

Maybe that was why I fell so hard for his game. Reggie was older, attractive, and funny. The kind of guy who knew all the right things to say and just how to say them. When I first saw him, he was flirting with some girl I knew from the neighborhood named Trisha. Trisha had a reputation, so it shouldn't have come as a surprise that she was hitting it off with Reggie. She usually hit it off with anything with the right amount of Y chromosomes (which is just a polite way of saying she was a ho). The surprise came when she left, and he turned his attention to me. He called them "free swimming lessons", but I know that for the lie it was. Back then I didn't realize the power I had in my body. How "Bag of Bones" could translate into something completely different in another man's eyes.

What stuck out the most, besides how smooth he was, was the ability he had to make me feel as if I were the center of the universe. His green-eyed gaze didn't help, though later I found out those were contacts. It was like Trisha had never existed for him, and I was all there was and ever would be.

It felt so damn good.

After that day at the pool, I couldn't stop thinking about him. Didn't want to stop thinking about him. He told me that he was eighteen and knowing I'd caught the eye of an older boy was a forbidden secret I kept close to the heart. The only people who knew about Reggie were Jade and Reggie's best friend, Keithan. Every chance we got, Jade and I would go over to Reggie's house to hang out and watch television. Reggie and Keithan would pick the two of us up in Reggie's car and drop us off hours later when it was time to get back home. During those stolen evenings, I found what I'd been looking for since I first came to DC—something of my own.

I loved hanging out with Reggie. He challenged me intellectually in a way that boys my own age couldn't. He listened to me and made me laugh. With just a look, Reggie could make me feel desired and sophisticated. For a fourteen-year-old, it was both terrifying and thrilling. I was a virgin at the time and determined to save myself until marriage. I was so used to being mocked for my beliefs that I worried what someone like Reggie would think if he found out. So, I kept the details to myself and basked in the glow that came from being desired.

Reggie had this ritual of inviting me back into his room whenever I came over to hang out. Each time I said no, preferring to stay in the living room and watch television with Jade and Keithan. I didn't know what lay in wait for me down that hall, but I knew instinctively that I wasn't ready for it. My dad was always lecturing me about boys and getting on my case about being on the phone too much, and I think that had a lot to do with my hesitance. Even so, in the end, it wasn't enough.

An orange tank top and black shorts.

I can remember what I was wearing like it was yesterday.

The day I was raped started off like any other. The only difference was that on that day, for whatever reason, I didn't turn down his invitation to come to his bedroom the way I usually did. We were lying spooning-style on his bed since there were no chairs in his bedroom. I was closest to the television set. When I first felt his cold hand trying to push through my jean shorts to pull down my panties, I said no. I even tried pushing him away. But he was strong. He had that kind of strength and persistence of will that only comes to light when you're a twenty-three-year-old man pretending to be a teenager and claiming something that isn't yours and doesn't want to be claimed. How was I supposed to stand up to that with my skinny arms and scared rabbit heart, beating so fast it nearly jumped out of my chest?

I didn't fight. I pathetically kept saying "no" and "stop" in a soft and trembling voice. Not the way they tell you you're supposed to fight in the movies. That desperate, sobbing, straining struggle for your life that makes you a true victim instead of just a girl who regretted her decisions. That's the part that haunted me the most. I wasn't the "perfect victim" (whoever that was). This violation was now Reggie's and, by extension, my secret. I coped by convincing myself that nothing terrible had happened to me at all. If it had been that bad, I would have fought harder. I would have screamed for help. Why hadn't I?

Why hadn't I stopped it?

Fast forward, I bit my bottom lip as another contraction rippled through my abdomen. The force of it dragged a groan from deep within me, and I realized with a start that I'd been holding my breath against the pain. Ordinarily, I'd be starting high school this year. In middle school I used to fantasize about what it would be like: the classes I would take, the friends I would make. High school had been a milestone on my way to college and independence. But instead of planning for my future, I was having a baby.

This was it. I was stepping into the danger zone. Oblivious to the hazard lights throwing a tantrum all around me. Clueless about what would come next and terrified of the unknown. I'd felt this way for so long that it was nearly impossible to remember a time when I wasn't petrified. The day I received the results of my pregnancy test, the lump in my throat had been so large that I was sure I'd choke on it.

"Positive."

The nurse's announcement had been without preamble or sympathy. She'd merely been stating a fact. It may have been just another workday for her, but for me, the news had opened the ground beneath my feet. Too frightened to think and too astonished to speak, it had been like being trapped in a nightmare. Teen pregnancy was a topic discussed in gym class, during the all-girl seminars. Oh sure, I sat up in class and nodded my head. I thought I perceived everything that was said, when the words spoken never seeped through my cloudy skull. I was only pretending as if I could wrap my mind around the picture the woman at the front of the room was painting. But hearing about it in class and living it were two different things. This wasn't supposed to be my life, and I waffled between feeling as if I'd been robbed and blaming myself for the theft. I, like many other teenagers, knew "it" happened, saw "it" happen, but nevertheless felt very distant to the fact that "it" could happen to me.

I was at a delicate age of innocence where thoughts I'd once considered to be immoral and wrong were just a natural part of growing up. I was getting familiar with being influenced by my peers. I was just beginning to experience things for myself and the shift in mindset made accepting what had happened to me even harder. As if overnight, I went from being "that Jesus freak" to the girl that everyone stared at from the corner of their eye and with their nostrils flared. I became the girl people whispered and wondered about. Without realizing it my peers, the very people I'd been so desperate to relate to, had become my judge, jury, and executioner. My peers and I, without any knowledge, established a love/hate relationship; they loved to hate me, and I hated loving them.

I was then a prime example of a pregnant adolescent.

Before Reggie, I'd been at the peak of curiosity about the secluded things in life. After him, I was shoved into an understanding of the world that had once been forbidden to me. It had been tainted by his violence and my own shame and guilt.

My first contraction had been an eye-opener. At first, I didn't understand what was happening. Then intuition took the reins, and my pulse went dashing for the gold. In that instance a plethora of emotion rippled through me: everything from denial, to regret, to a fierce desire for vengeance. But all of it, even my desire to punish Reggie for what happened that day, took a backseat to terror.

No, I'd thought, *I'm not ready. This isn't fair. I can't give birth to a baby when I'm still just a child myself.*

A child, yes, but my innocence had been spoiled. I felt cheated, as if I'd been duped by an expert at a poker game. He must have found me an easy target to manipulate. Thanks to my own naivete and childlike vulnerability, I'd gotten myself knocked up by a cruel, uncaring, deserting, irresponsible, pathetic, poor excuse of a black man. He'd better pray my wishes didn't come true. On the wave of another contraction, I cursed that Don Giovanni (Casanova) impotent.

If there's any justice in this world at all, he'll never get it up again.

Being bashful, I almost missed out on having my baby in a delivery room. The night before, I experienced a sporadic, unpleasant, rippling sensation but didn't tell a soul. Instead, I sat on the toilet until each spell proved itself a false alarm. I finally managed to coax myself to sleep, but the next morning, the pressure was back and stronger than ever. It was intense enough to wake me up, so the first thing I did was read the pamphlet that I'd collected from the clinic. From it, I learned that when in labor walking would increase the contractions. The problem was that every time the idea would try to creep into my mind, I would knock it right back down. I couldn't be going into labor because that would mean that this was actually happening. That there really was no going back. Even up until that moment, I was able to convince myself that it wasn't quite real.

Acknowledging the fact that I was in labor would turn the idea of a baby from a thought into a reality. I kept pacing from my room to the bathroom, and after the tenth trip, I could no longer ignore the source of my restlessness. I'd go to the hospital, I reasoned. They'd tell me that I was constipated or gassy and that would be the end of it. By the time I finally broke down and headed to the ER, it was 3:30 in the afternoon. I asked my big brother for two dollars to get on the bus. Since it was the second week of January, the weather was cold, windy, and raining enough to mind. Somehow, I managed to defeat the commute to the bus stop. It was only a quarter of a block away and across the street from my home, but the trip felt longer thanks to the discomfort in my middle.

While I was standing at the bus stop trying to balance my unruly umbrella against the wind and wet, my luck went out of character for a brief time. An acquaintance pulled up just as the bus arrived. I took the risk of letting the bus pass, just to ask him if he would take me to the hospital. To my relief, he said yes. Once in the passenger seat, I realized that my luck was returning to its old ways once again. Everything seemed to entice the unmanageable discomfort: the rain, the wind, the umbrella, and especially the obnoxious conversation he produced on the way to the hospital. He'd hit on me once, months before, and was cocky enough to assume that my pregnancy was the reason I'd turned him down.

"If you'd just told me sooner, I would have understood."

Consciously, I heard him but tried my best to ignore him. There were more important things on my mind than his hurt feelings and as far as I was concerned, messing with him would have put me in the exact same position I was in now. Over the past few months, I'd come to a realization: most men felt entitled to a woman's attention and her reaction. I couldn't just ignore his advances, and my honest disinterest wasn't a valid enough reason to take "no" for an answer.

So, when he persisted, I gave him a semblance of a response:

"You're nothing but a chump," I'd told him, too agitated to be nervous or polite. "I sat in your living room while I was eight months pregnant and you didn't even realize what was going on until I told you just a few minutes ago." My lip curled in disgust. "You're inattentive and self-centered, and I've had enough of both to last me a lifetime." The nerve of him, to expect me to have an interest when he'd failed to show me anything interesting.

Idiot. I was only happy of his existence for the ride. We finally reached DC General Hospital and my egotistical hero gave me his phone number and asked me to call him. He was so sure of himself. I suspected that he thought he'd be the ideal substitute father. If his goal had been to convince me of his worth, he'd failed miserably. Each of these minor events led me to foresee that I had, in the depths of my heart, developed a hatred for men.

I was totally humiliated once I arrived in the emergency room. The doctors' diagnosis was that I was about to have my baby. This was happening whether I was ready or not. They relocated me to the delivery room at 5:00 p.m. My accommodations were a disappointment; the windowless, coldly sterile room wasn't even an imitation of what I'd imagined. A small radio sounded off from the corner. Rather than offer comfort, the music only reminded me of how lonely I was.

Boom!

Another contraction hit like a freight train, and I prayed for sleep. If I were unconscious, at least I wouldn't have to feel any pain. I begged for something, anything, to take it away but they refused to give me an epidermal. Prenatal care hadn't prepared me for actual delivery, and at some point, I started to sob. Unsure of what to anticipate but confident that this would break me. My body felt like a strange atmosphere. I was dehydrated, and my lips became the factory for starch. I licked, and the dryness would automatically reproduce. My back, the pain in my back was torture! If I had been intoxicated to the highest degree, the pain in my back would have made me sober.

I started pulling my hair, trying to focus on the pain in my scalp instead. At least that was something I could control. It worked, but barely. I lay on the hospital bed, legs cocked open, as the doctor came by to examine me every two minutes. My water didn't break naturally; they had to stick something in me for that. The nurses complained that I was too loud, that I would upset the other patients, but no matter how hard I tried I couldn't seem to bite back my cries.

My ears were betraying me. I kept hearing "Don't push!" but that couldn't be right. Try telling a dog not to bark knowing it was his only form of communication or a drowning man not to gasp for air. It was in my nature. Irrevocable and unavoidable. The urge to push was all that I was. At one point, I must have snapped because the stranger, also known as the doctor, that was delivering my baby had the nerve to tell me, "Don't take your frustration out on me. I'm not the one that gotcha pregnant."

That was the stamp on the package. I hated men. The suspicion that had been growing in the back of my mind during the ride to the hospital had just been confirmed. I hated men. Not all of them *were* Reggie, but it didn't matter because any of them *could* have been. They had the power to hurt, to cut me down, with either words or actions, and I despised them for it. After thirty minutes crawled along, feeling like an eternity, they unbelievably gave me permission to push.

I did. With everything in me. I pushed until I felt something give. The head. She was on her way, and I was nearly tapped out. I gathered the tattered remains of my strength and pushed again, straining what little fractions remained of myself to the breaking point, until with a "pop" she tumbled into the world.

Never again, I swore to myself.

Then I saw her.

I didn't know what the future would hold for the two of us. All I knew for sure was that I could smell her, the scent of her skin made my mouth water and my breasts ache. I wanted to hold her, to feed her, to breath her deep into my lungs and never let go. This creature, small and mewling, had been born of my flesh and already I couldn't imagine ever letting her go. I couldn't believe it! I'd given birth to a baby girl. God gives what is deserved. I had a baby girl to raise hell to me like I did to my parents. Before I would have the chance to adjust to the fact, she would be a teenager.

I have an interesting future to look forward to—parenthood.

They handed her to me, my baby, my China, wrapped in a yellow receiving blanket. Her oriental black, curly hair enveloped the crease of her knitted yellow hat. She was already making a fashion statement. As I embraced her, tears of joy intermingled with tears of sadness challenged one another in a slow race down my cheeks. My dark hands were trembling as I gripped her. She was so pale, so fragile, I was afraid she might shatter in my arms. I was so nervous as I entertained the thought that I might be holding her too loose, or even too tight.

The love that I felt towards her could have filled infinity, and I would have still had enough left over for a forever. I had no words to describe the emotion that rocked through me the moment I held her against my breast, skin to skin. She was all mine. All six pounds and five ounces of her. I could see myself in her already, just as I could see traces of her father. Despite the violence of her conception, I knew that I'd been blessed. I was young, but my fate was destined rich because I already possessed the most valuable treasure in the world. I decided I would give everyone something else to talk about; I would be the best mother I could be.

In the recovery room, I found the peace I'd been craving. I was exhausted. As weak as Popeye before he eats his spinach. But my thoughts were racing, and I couldn't sleep. There was one thought that stuck out the most.

I'd never have an experience that could possibly compete with this moment. Giving birth had to be the most beautiful thing in the world.

REFLECTIONS

Now I know the things I didn't know back then. For one, a lesson is well taught through experience. I'd ignored my dad's rules, ignored my own values, and all for what? To have the attention of a predator who would eventually hurt me more than I'd ever been hurt before. At the age when I assumed, I wasn't supposed to take life seriously, I was raped. In one callous act, all the inherent opportunities associated with being a teenager, with having my entire life ahead of me, had been thrown into question. Girls my age had sex all the time and got away with it so why was I the one who was being punished?

While it may not have been fair, the experience did teach me things about myself.

I learned, for example, that I don't break, that I wasn't spoiled, and that I damn sure wasn't weak. Most importantly, that I was responsible for how long I allowed what hurt me to continue to haunt me. This was part of my journey of becoming who I am. Because of what happened, my daughter and I overcame many of life's obstacles together and came out on top. Back then, I understood that I could wallow in self-pity or I could take responsibility for my part in the direction my life had gone. It took decades before these realizations would occur to me, and by then I had enough knowledge to fill a bag, or a suitcase, or…

A purse.

If I could condense everything I'd learned as a woman, and as a psychotherapist and social worker, into a single space, I would choose a purse. Or, more accurately, the contents within that purse. They vary in size, shape, and color but we all have one. Usually, we keep it wrapped close, and we never go anywhere without its familiar weight. It lies, a comforting presence across our hearts, bouncing against our wombs and dancing around our hips as we strut through life. It's by our side through every tragedy and triumph, and it holds everything essential to our journey through this world.

Here, I want you to have this.

A spiritual, emotional purse full of insight, wisdom, and strength. Something you can carry with you always and use as a shield against the relationships in your life that are breaking you down and tearing you apart. I created these lessons so that you could pull them forth at a moment's notice when temptation and years of bad habits cajole and whisper for you to travel a road already well-worn by regret and tears. Years spent in one bad relationship after another have gifted me with pearls of wisdom, and now, I gift them to you. Use this gift as you create and maintain a healthy, harmonious, and loving romantic relationship!

Chapter 3: *The Mirror*

A REFLECTION OF THE TRUTH

> *I have learned that as long as I hold fast to my beliefs and values—and follow my own moral compass—then the only expectations I need to live up to are my own.*
> *—Michelle Obama*

When you pull out that compact mirror, what are your intentions? Who do you expect to see? Every single time, without exception, that mirror will reflect to you–you. The compact mirror in your purse represents your values, providing a true reflection of who you really are.

I want to make one thing clear: *For all his tough talk and uncompromising nature, my dad loved my daughter.*

I still remember the first time he held his granddaughter and the way his features softened. The gentleness with which he cradled her tiny head. The awe. When I was growing up, I'd thought he was too strict. I remember one day I was walking from the grocery store to the car and as soon as I climbed into the backseat, he lit into me about the way that I'd carried myself across the parking lot. Looking back, I wonder now if that moment was just his crotchety way of worrying about me. He did that a lot. If I was on the phone for too long or if my clothes fit a little too well, he'd have something to say about it. The man was the definition of strict. He was also old-fashioned and insensitive. In a lot of ways, it was as if he were overcompensating for my mother's admittedly lax parenting. In those moments, I felt like he criticized me every chance that he got, but later realized he also pushed me to be the best version of myself. Dad encouraged me to stick with school and make a better life for myself and my daughter.

My parents weren't perfect, no one is, but they taught me things that I didn't fully appreciate until I was grown with two kids of my own. Whatever his faults, my dad was unshakable when it came to his values, and his stalwart nature stuck with me. It was like he was made of stone, if the stone was a black man with a short temper and a big voice.

But that same stubbornness that I admire now is what made me shy away as a kid. I knew he wouldn't approve of me seeing Reggie, so I didn't tell him. I justified it by saying that Reggie and I were just kicking it, and that nothing sexual would happen. Like a lot of teenagers who rebel against their parents' wisdom, I thought I knew better and had everything under control. Totally false! I ignored the values that he'd set in place for my own protection, the same way that I ignored my personal beliefs all in an effort to fit in and be accepted.

During the years I've worked as a social worker and licensed therapist, I've seen hundreds of clients (mostly women) who have done the exact same thing. They give up part of themselves for a chance at love. And I get it, I really do. It seems like everywhere we look there are more horror stories about broken people in broken relationships. According to recent statistics, the divorce rate in the United States might be dropping, but fewer and fewer people are getting married. Black couples especially seem to have a hard time. Between the stereotype of the absentee father and disproportionate levels of incarceration versus population, the idea of the "single, black female" is a prevalent one. When we aren't being hypersexualized and fetishized by the media, we are forced to be strong.

Let me tell you. Having the world expect you to stay strong despite whatever abuse, misogyny, ridicule, and heartache is thrown your way is a cruel burden to bear. If you become justifiably upset, you run the risk of stepping into another, equally noxious role: that of the angry black woman. As a result, many black women put up with more than they should from their partners, often finding themselves trying to be a "ride or die" to prove their loyalty (and as a direct result) their worth.

Women from all races have internalized this idea that in order to be happy, we must first suffer. That to prove ourselves as devoted, we must put up with being treated like dirt by our partners. Apparently, the law of equivalent exchange doesn't just apply to alchemists and chemists. But gaining something by losing something of equal value is not a concept that should be applied to love and romance.

Whenever a client comes to me with relationship problems, I ask them a simple question:

If you were an accountant, would your significant other always be making a deposit or a withdrawal? Do they enhance your relationship? Are they invested in you? Or are they always taking? Your pride, your sense of safety, your concept of self. What do you find yourself sacrificing in order to remain in a relationship you know deep down isn't working?

Before getting involved with anyone, it's important to first understand who you are and what you want. That's where taking a look at your own reflection comes into play. When you give up on your values, you're no longer reflecting yourself, but who you are with the person you're in a relationship with.

So why do we do it?

For some of us, it's lack of self-esteem or confidence. For others, it's a matter of convenience or even happenstance. The "why" isn't nearly as important as the "when." *When* are you going to step aside and let go of something that no longer serves you? *When* will you admit to yourself that you not only deserve better, but *want* better?

Every encounter you have, every relationship you're in, either invests something into you or takes something away. The more toxicity that surrounds you, the more of you gets erased. You are a rock at the center of a raging river; your proud edges get worn down and chipped off over time until you're reshaped into something more convenient for the river than the rock. Just like that rock, you leave pieces of yourself behind with every person that you meet. Whether it's emotional or physical abuse, chronic cheating, or being lied to, manipulated, used up, and taken advantage of what you accept from one partner subconsciously lays the groundwork for what you'll accept from the next.

Once you lay aside your values, you've erased the line in the sand that demands respect, loyalty, and kindness. Not only for the men (or women) in your life, but for yourself. Each blow chisels away at your self-esteem until the woman you see in the mirror is unrecognizable from who you once were and who you may be striving to be.

For a long time, I wasn't "Montrella Cowan, beautiful, intelligent, and driven." Instead, I was "Montrella, the victim and single mother defiled and weak." I allowed my experiences to shape my view of myself and compromised the values that had once given me strength and purpose.

It was a dangerous combination and one that dictated what I searched for in men. The most frightening part was that I didn't even realize that I was doing it. The men I knew after Reggie were no better than he was in many ways because I didn't think that I deserved any better. Years later I can look back and recognize my behavior for what it was: a symptom of my assault that only grew worse the longer I went without getting help. Because of my past hurt, I was constantly attracting the same—or equally toxic—relationships. My standards for determining desirable behavior were so low that they were basically nonexistent.

It's like a woman who's used to being physically abused finally finding a partner who doesn't beat her but mentally and emotionally tears her down every day. Her mindset is that she may not be happy, but "he's never raised a hand to me." The woman she sees reflected is someone who lacks something fundamental. After all, why else would all the men in her life say or do these things to hurt her, unless there was something wrong with her?

There are several reasons why women stay in bad relationships. Some stay for their kids, others because they don't feel as if they'll be able to find better. Some are haunted by this false idea that time is working against them, and that they will soon be too old to attract a great guy. A few don't see anything wrong with their partner's dysfunctional behavior, mainly because they've seen it all before. Regardless of why, the result remains the same.

You need to make a change.

Change, like anything worthwhile, requires hard work and that hard work starts at the source. Instead of getting caught up in the idea of being in a relationship regardless of the personal cost, focus instead on identifying the values you consider the most important. There's no secret formula to finding fulfillment, but with the correct ingredients you can start off on the right path.

RECIPE #1 - The "Do No Harm, but Take No Crap" Casserole

Have you lost your sense of self? Do you feel as if the people in your life are always walking all over you? Do you find it impossible to fight for and express your own needs and desires? The Do No Harm but Take No Crap Casserole is perfect for the modern woman trying to reconnect with her inner Boss.

Prep Time: Varies   Serving Size: 1

<u>**Directions:**</u>
1. List at least 50 traits you're looking for in a significant other.
2. Write down who you are—List faults as well as positive attributes.
3. Now, on a separate piece of paper write down who you need to become to attract that ideal significant other you described above. Do these two things coincide or clash? Where do they overlap?
4. Make a note of what changes you need to make in your life to go from Point A to Point B. Remember, the more specific, the better. Be honest with yourself.
5. Acknowledge who you become within a relationship. How different are you from the woman you ideally want to be? Why?
6. Note how who you are within a relationship affects the other connections in your life—Our Spirituality, family, friends, and work relationships are all intertwined. How does one affect all the others? Is it positive or negative?
7. Pick your top four values. These are things that you refuse to compromise on or set aside.
8. Accept that struggle and conflict in a relationship arise when you sacrifice those values. Remember that knowledge is power, only when APPLIED.

Additional Notes (Repeat daily or as often as needed. Mix well and marinate.):
"I am worthy of a life filled with love, respect, and happiness.

~ I have the power and responsibility to lay claim to and manifest my own values, truth, and purpose.

~ I am deserving of love from myself and others.

~ I know that I deserve only the best.

~ I give and receive love easily.

~ I am willing to be vulnerable."

Nutritional Facts - Per Serving
- 40% Take No Crap
- 21% Inner Peace
- 0% Salt
- 30% Strong Sense of Self-Worth
- 9% Glow

10/10 - Would Recommend

~ *Reconnect with your inner BOSS!* ~

Chapter 4: *Seth*

My rape and subsequent pregnancy turned into a game of "He said, she said." It wasn't until after my daughter was born that I learned that Reggie was actually a 23-year-old man. Considering everything he'd done, the fact that he was a liar shouldn't have fazed me, but it was yet another blow. You see, Reggie's age was one of the reasons he denied ever laying a finger on me. It wasn't a question of whether or not our encounter had been consensual—it was whether it had taken place at all. His refusal to claim his daughter had just as much to do with the kind of person he was as it did the fact that he didn't want to get slapped with a statutory rape charge.

The weeks and months that followed were some of the hardest I'd ever had to endure. I was getting used to being a new mother, going to school, and trying to juggle the physical and mental fallout that came with ever having laid eyes on Reggie in the first place. The emotional roller coaster of seeing my daughter in my arms brought me as high as I'd ever been, while the constant reminder of how she'd come to exist in the first place was an albatross around my neck, dragging me down and leaving me there to drown.

According to the CDC, approximately 8.7% of women and 5.3% of men have depression. Which, if you're no good at math, pans out to over 300 million people around the world. And the number continues to grow as time passes. Suicide is the tenth leading cause of death in the United States, with over 47,000 Americans dying each year. This includes children and adolescents since 3% of children between the ages of six and twelve suffer from major depression disorder.[3]

There's no telling if I would have struggled with depression had Reggie left me to my own devices. Sexual assault can be a catalyst, but it's by no means the only form of trauma I was experiencing at the time and eventually had to work through. My mother's drug addiction and codependency, the generational poverty that shaped most of my childhood and young adult life and dealing with the foster care system. Being physically and emotionally isolated from friends and family, the grief and loss that accompanied the forced loss of my virginity.

None of this even considers what I went through after I became an adult. It was so much to chew on that sometimes I was afraid I would choke on it if not for my faith and determination to see the light at the other side of an otherwise too long tunnel. While the birth of my daughter gave me someone and something to fight for, there were also times when having a child so young felt like a load I'd never be able to bear.

One in every seven women will go through postpartum depression. You're more likely to experience it if you've had depression before, but over half of those who develop it have never shown any signs of depression at all. Depression sunk its claws into me early and I was never able to shake it completely loose. Of course, I want to say that it all got easier over time and, in many ways, that's true. But healing is never a linear process. There was no secret formula to overcoming the trauma I'd experienced. In fact, much of my healing consisted of a lot of back and forth. For every moment of

---

[3] Available at: https://www.cdc.gov/nchs/products/databriefs/db303.htm.

progress, there were several setbacks. The tricky part was that I was never sure when I would find myself reacting to my pain instead of growing from it. There are a lot of women who have found themselves in my exact position. While I didn't experience the same type of trauma as an adult that I had as a child, it was still shaping my life in ways that I could never fathom.

It's said that if someone experiences physical or emotional abuse when they're young, then they're more likely to end up in relationships that mirror that abuse. Why is that? Do we gravitate towards what we know? Is it instinctive to place ourselves in harm's way when hurt is the only language we speak? Or maybe, as was often the case with me, repeating that cycle of trauma and abuse wasn't a choice I made but one that was made for me.

I was groomed to be a victim from an early age. It made me more susceptible to the manipulations of men who knew what to look for and how to exploit it to get what they wanted. I was blind to the machinations around me because I had never been trained to see them. Growing up, my faith in people had been something given at face value. I had to learn the hard way that not everyone has your heart and where I could look at someone in my position and want to heal, someone else could look at that same person and want to take.

Reggie was my first encounter with this, but not my last. And, no matter how much I might have wanted to forget that day, my daughter's birth made that impossible. She was a living, breathing tether to him and there was nothing I could do to change that. Despite his denial, I rejected the idea of her not having her father as a figure in her life. My dad had taken on the role of savior thanks to my mom's battle with addiction. Because of that, the archetype of the "Father" became an essential role to fill. The years I'd spent without my own had left me with the belief that a girl needed her dad. I always wanted the best for my children. As the years passed,

I reached out to Reggie on multiple occasions to try and force him to take his responsibilities seriously. I didn't want money from him, but I was determined to make him step up as a father.

If you're wondering how and why I would want to try to co-parent with the man who'd assaulted me, the answer is simple. I blamed myself for my rape more than I did Reggie. The shame was a burden that I bore all alone, and the more time that passed, the easier it was to convince myself that the needs of my daughter outweighed my own.

I didn't want to accept what had been done to me. I didn't even want to give it a name. Rape was something that happened to other people, not me. Maybe I just hadn't understood what was happening? Maybe it had hurt so much because I just hadn't gotten into it the way I should have? Maybe...maybe I'd wanted it? My understanding of what "rape" was didn't mesh with what had happened to me. But regardless of how often I tried to justify these feelings, nothing could erase the sense of violation that assailed me whenever I spoke Reggie's name, or saw his face, or closed my eyes. I wanted that feeling to go away, I wanted to feel normal, and the only way I knew how to do that was to sweep the shadows of that day aside and paint myself an all-new memory. A memory in which I was the willing, albeit ignorant, coquette. In this new version of events, Reggie didn't overpower me or ignore my cries. In this alternate universe of my own making, it was regret that I hadn't stuck with my plans to wait until after marriage that haunted me.

"Rape" was a monster hiding beneath my bed and I burrowed my head beneath the covers, tucked its name close to my chest so I wouldn't have to speak it aloud, and waited for the sun to come up on a new day.

I kept that mindset for the next six years.

By the time I turned eighteen, I had a job and my own apartment. My relationship with my stepmother and siblings hadn't improved after I gave birth. If anything, the vitriol between us all grew even more pronounced. It wasn't just that I was a reminder of my dad's cheating either. My stepmom and I were two fundamentally different people. She was a woman that lived in fear; she'd never learned how to drive and had never held a real job. She was always talking about moving out of Southeast DC, where there was astounding poverty and violence, but talking was all she ever did.

By comparison, I didn't shy away from hard work and I was always hungry to learn and do more. I was everything she wished she could be. I represented her lost youth and squandered opportunities, and she hated me for it. So, shortly after my birthday, I found myself living on my own. As a single mother, I worked long hours to provide for myself and my daughter. Between my job and raising my daughter, I didn't have time for anything else unless I made a conscious effort to set some aside. Which was why, when my aunt flew in from New York for Unifest in 1999, I made sure to help at her booth on my day off.

Unifest is a multicultural event held every year in Anacostia sponsored by the church I was a member of at the time. A local DJ provides music and there are family-friendly activities and lots of food. Hundreds of merchants take advantage of the influx of people coming into town to sell their wares and my aunt decided to take part in the festivities. My aunt, who was my mom's youngest sister, had always been a deeply religious woman, something we had in common. It was nice having someone I could finally relate to on that front and I enjoyed her company even though it was sweltering out and I was tired. The day I met Seth, we were selling some of the clothes, shoes, and hats my aunt had brought with her from New York. He spotted me in the crowd and strolled up, eventually pulling me aside to talk.

That first encounter set the tone for our entire relationship.

Considering what I know now, it seems disingenuous to name him after an Egyptian god. You have to understand though; at the time it fit. He had a mysteriousness about him that was attractive to me. The black wife-beater he wore made it obvious that he worked out a lot. He had an eight-pack, shoulder-length locks, and an intensity that drew me in. He was one of those confident black men who marched through the world as if he understood it in a way the rest of us couldn't. The kind of black man that preached about the motherland and the power inherent in the DNA of his beautiful black sisters. The icing on the cake when it came to this "king" was that he had his son with him. His son was the same age as my daughter, so you couldn't tell me they were not godsent at the time.

In Seth's eyes he was a King, and he was intent on finding his Queen in yours truly. In reality, any of the women out and about that day would have probably fit the bill. He was a womanizer after all, and it was in his nature to cast his line and see what he could catch. On a hot summer day, with reggae blasting in the air around us, and sweat on our skin, I just happened to be the one to take the bait.

It helped that he'd brought his son with him.

I wasn't especially trusting or open when it came to men. Not after Reggie. So, the fact that Seth had a son, Khalid, around the same age as China did a lot to put me at ease. It transformed him from just a guy spitting game into a Father. Someone attractive, reliable, and good with kids. Some men shied away from dating a young mother, but my situation didn't seem to faze him in the slightest. Seth was a smooth talker, a lot like Reggie had been, and I had a weakness for smooth talkers.

Growing up, learning had always been my passion. Even now, I go through life with the heart of a student and the soul of an explorer. Seth appealed to that part of me. He was ten years older, handsome, and opened my eyes to all sorts of new experiences those first few magical months of courting.

On our first date, he invited my daughter and me to a vegan market run by Hebrew Israelites. It catered to an Afrocentric, fully organic lifestyle complete with almond milk and tofu. We ate soy ice cream with our kids while he told me about how Jesus was black, and the Pharaohs used to rock dreads. I'd never heard anything like it before, and before the date was over, I was in complete awe of him. This man was a free thinker, independent, charismatic, and seemingly intelligent. He wasn't shy about telling it like it was. For a woman who didn't even know what veganism was at the time, for someone who'd spent her life relatively sheltered but always questioning life's quirks, talking to Seth was like peeking inside of Pandora's box. Seth knew secrets, he understood what made the world tick, and I was hungry to absorb as much as I could from him.

His mind wasn't the only thing that drew me in, however. Like I said, the man was built and beautiful. I shouldn't have to tell you the kind of warning signs a woman is willing to ignore when a man is toned in all the right places and hung like a horse. But while Seth might have seemed like the perfect man for me, there were a few things that gave me pause.

For one, he had two kids besides Khalid. All by different women. He also didn't have a job. It was hard to be antiestablishment while working a nine-to-five and Seth was nothing if not fully committed to not being committed to anything.

But we'll get into that later.

My aunt told me once that she knew that Seth wouldn't be any good for me because he'd been a distraction from day one. She wasn't wrong, but I couldn't escape the feeling that God had put him in my path. Before meeting him, I'd prayed for God to place a man like him in my life. The timing was just too perfect to be anything but divine intervention. Besides, raising my daughter on my own was hard, and I was mentally and emotionally drained. Trying to get Reggie to step up was a constant battle, and I needed someone in my life that I could count on.

I thought (hoped) that Seth would be that someone.

For a little while, he was. He taught me about simple things like reading the ingredients while grocery shopping and about the benefits of being a conscious eater, which led me on my fifteen-year journey of changing my diet and becoming vegan. From the first day we met, he took the reins, and I was just along for the ride. The combination of his age, strength, and seeming intelligence translated into authority and I fell in line without a second thought. I felt I had finally found my King. It wasn't until years later that I would realize his marketing was far better than the contents of his package. He even had a stutter that he hid from me for years. I just thought the brother took long pauses, being so deep and all. Another thing I discovered is that he lied about his birth origin. He told me he was from New Jersey, but in fact was born and bred in Virginia. Later he admitted that he was conceived in New Jersey. He was so misleading; it was a joke.

I invited him to church once. He lived close by so even though he did have a car to get around, it would have been easy enough for him to walk there. He turned me down. I can remember the almost condescending smile on his face when he shook his head no.

"Why not?"

"I'll explain it to you later."

According to Seth, all religion was slavery, though that didn't stop him from taking from different belief systems to justify his various sins and vices. He believed only in what benefitted him, when it benefitted him, and that carried over into other areas of his life. If someone wasn't useful or, God forbid, went against his rules, then they didn't deserve a place in his life.

It may be hard to believe, but he was my everything. I spent hours listening to him preach about the white man and broken systems and how the corruption in the church ran too deeply to ever be eradicated. He opened my eyes to so many things, but that wasn't always a good thing. All too soon, the support system I'd managed to build around my daughter and me after her birth began to clash with the dynamics that made up my relationship with Seth. My aunt had picked up how controlling he was from the beginning, and because of my growing distrust and apathy towards religion, it caused a rift between the two of us.

Months after Seth and I started dating, the rest of my family and friends all met similar fates. I was isolated from my loved ones and set adrift. Seth's mission was accomplished. The only one left standing in the aftermath was the very man who'd been the cause of the chaos in the first place.

Being the hypocrite that he was, I should not have been surprised to discover that Seth was a hustler, selling drugs to his community members without discrimination of age, race, or gender. I found out in stages that he was selling weed to make ends meet. First, I noticed the constant scent of marijuana even when he was not medicating himself with it by lighting up a joint. The stench would be stronger in certain parts of his house like the kitchen, but it was always a constant odor combined with all the incense he would burn throughout the day. Another clue was the inconsistent but regular traffic. Yep, strangers would come to his door and call his phone at all hours of the day and night. Being from the projects in Brooklyn, drug dealers and how they manage their activities were not foreign to me. But it was the day that some guys tried to rob Seth that the truth came to light. Seth came clean and admitted to distributing and was shocked when I admitted that it hadn't been hard to figure out. That just showed how naïve he thought I was. Even after those robbers left bullet holes in the front door of Seth's apartment.

Notwithstanding, Seth convinced me to let him move into my apartment. He said that staying at his crib was no longer an option. I'm sure that it was his fear that the robbers would come back, or perhaps it was him manipulating me; maybe it was a combination of both. Either way his goal had been achieved once again. Since I was cut off from friends and family and needed a helping hand with my daughter, I agreed; if he stopped selling, he could stay. I wouldn't tolerate him putting either my daughter or me at risk.

That was the agreement.

Like everything else that came out of Seth's mouth, it turned out to be a load of bull. He kept selling even after we were together and the fact that he'd broken his word was the topic of some of our many arguments. When we first got together, I was working full-time at an internationally recognized hotel chain. It was a good job and soon after I started, I was promoted to supervisor. I was there for three years, and was very successful during that time, before my frequent arguments with Seth outside of work got me laid off.

This was a low point in my life. While the sex was good, it didn't fulfill me. There was still something missing, and if anything, the loneliness that I'd always felt only seemed to grow worse. There was something disheartening about sleeping next to someone and feeling as if you might as well be in the bed with a stranger for all the comfort you found in their presence. I started to see the pattern in the timing. When Seth wanted to step out and cheat on me, he would create an upset, knowing that I would put him out. He knew all the right things to say and do when he wanted back in too. I fell for his tricks for too long. Between the constant fights and the overbearing rules of the house, depression began sinking its claws into me. I coped the best way I knew how: by writing in my journal. It was my one and only outlet.

My one freedom.

Seth went behind my back and read it one day. It takes a certain amount of callousness to use someone's emotions to manipulate them into doing what you want, but he never even hesitated. Maybe I wouldn't have minded playing his head games if I had been his only target, but not even my daughter was safe from his machinations.

Seth controlled every aspect of our lives. Our home had become his impromptu kingdom, and his word was law. I gave up wearing my hair loose or in braids and got my hair and my daughter's hair locked. I changed the way that I dressed because he didn't want me conforming to "Eurocentric standards of beauty." The same was the case for my daughter and Khalid, who lived with us too. Seth insisted that my daughter attend the same Afrocentric school as Khalid. A school where the philosophy was something he could mostly agree with—I say "mostly" because it would not be Seth if he couldn't find points of disagreement with everything and everyone. The school only served vegan food and the students were required to wear African attire.

On top of nitpicking at our appearance, none of us could eat anything unless it was completely vegan. This was especially hard for my daughter, because she had to give up a lot of her favorite foods. On top of that, she was still growing and needed more nutrients than his stringent diet could account for. She was only six years old when Seth began running the household like his own little dictatorship, so she didn't understand what was happening and why.

It was around this time that I decided to finally confront Reggie.

I brought my daughter with me back to his apartment building in the 'hood of Northeast DC and knocked on the front door. I was surprised when he answered, but my astonishment paled in comparison to his own when he saw our daughter with me. He spent so many years denying her. On the one hand, forcing Reggie to spend time with his daughter gave her a much-needed break from the drama at home. On the other hand, Reggie went out of his way to break Seth's rules every chance he got. He didn't like the other man even though they'd never met and didn't approve of anything he stood for. Reggie became China's saving grace because whenever she visited, she had carte blanche to do whatever the hell she wanted. It was Reggie's way of wooing her loyalty, and I didn't realize until it was too late that I'd given him all the ammunition he needed to turn her against me. Reggie's goal was to find a loophole to paying child support, which he had managed to evade 95% of the time up to this point.

Seth and I were never constant. We broke up and got back together several times in the four years we were dating. Each time I thought I was over him, then he would reel me back in. For me, there was no defining moment, no straw that finally broke the back of the proverbial camel. Instead, my resolve to get him out of my life was a culmination of weeks and months of self-reflection and soul-searching. Who was I? The question reared its head when I least expected it. Every woman he cheated on me with, every put-down, and every rule I was forced to follow made the words echo in my mind with a growing intensity that was impossible to ignore.

Who am I?

I no longer recognized myself. Who was this woman I had become?

There should have been enough time for me to figure that out, but true to form, Seth never gave me that opportunity. I was contemplating leaving him when I found out that I was pregnant with my second child. At the time, that was my only other pregnancy since giving birth to my daughter.

I was struggling to pay bills, trapped in a demoralizing relationship, and growing increasingly depressed. I knew that I didn't want to stay with Seth, but I wasn't sure how to walk away. Seth was my first serious relationship. Seth was the first grown-up relationship I had, even though he fell short of the qualities I'd always found important. I'd put so much time and effort into holding our family together, had given up so much of myself to live up to his standards, that it seemed wrong to just throw it away even if he was a drain on my resources and energy. Like Reggie, I believed that Seth's failures were more my fault than his. If I just worked a little harder, things would be better for all of us.

Speaking of work, Seth had long since convinced me to leave the corporate world where I could earn an honest living. He had trained me to be rebellious towards "the white man's system." With his hypocrisy, he was OK with us being on welfare, though it was not enough to get us through even half of the month. Under the spell of his influence, I got fired from the hospitality industry, from a job I loved so much and which valued my leadership, where I had invested three and a half years of my life, and had climbed the ranks at such a young age. Shortly thereafter, I got another job closer to my home. That job, in the sales department of the hospitality industry of a smaller hotel chain, didn't last long. If fact, with Seth in my life, it only lasted six months. Not only was I wearing a head wrap to hide the hideous unmaintained locks that were not favored in the workplace, but Seth would terrorize me on the way to work every morning by driving three times the speed limit. I felt like shit. I resorted to driving a taxicab. This was supposed to allow me to have that "freedom" that Seth always spoke about. The fact is that I was about one of four women cabdrivers in DC—and I was definitely the youngest of them. As a cabdriver I had good days and bad days, and there were no benefits for the self-employed. The control over my life was slipping away.

I was trapped in the mindset that "struggle love" was the only kind of love worth finding. Like many black women, society had taught me that giving up on my man while he was struggling was a mark of a weak woman. Black women were strong, we were sassy, we were sexual; at least that's how the media portrayed us. I wish I had known back then that black girls deserved health over toxicity, and that we aren't obligated to "hold it down" at the expense of our own peace. I didn't realize that being his "ride or die" was a choice.

The responsibility for solving all our issues always fell to me because Seth would never bother to put forth that kind of effort when he could just blame someone else. So, realizing that I was pregnant again was like a punch to the gut. I was already stretched thin taking care of China, Seth, and his son. This was my second pregnancy, and while I didn't want to marry Seth the way he insisted, I did see my baby as a sign of better things to come. I would finally have the chance to do all the things I had missed out on with my firstborn. I loved my daughter but considering the trauma I was going through at the time it was no wonder the weeks and months leading up to her birth were riddled with anger and shame. Maybe my desire to create a better future for myself and China was giving me some much-needed strength and courage, but I decided to see the pregnancy through to term.

It was the best decision I have ever made.

Just as my pregnancy with my daughter reflected where I was emotionally and spiritually after my attack, the way I handled my pregnancy with my son seemed to correspond with my budding maturity. There was something about my second child that demanded more from my spirit. I was no longer content to struggle through life with Seth. There was more out there, and I wanted to experience it all. I was no longer willing to accept less than what I deserved. By the time my son was born, I wanted both of my children to be in a position where they could grow and prosper. My goal was to give them both all the opportunities that I had lacked growing up and I couldn't see that coming to fruition with Seth dragging us all down. For all his talk of progression, Seth was as stuck in his ways as my stepmother had been. He liked to pretend as if he were a forward thinker, a modern-day philosopher, when in truth he was stagnated. The saddest part was that he didn't see that he was his own worst enemy. Seth was the kind of man who put on a good show, but when you peeked behind the curtain there was nothing there. He didn't have a real job the entire time I knew him, and he walked or rode his bike everywhere because he didn't own a car. He was an expert at hiding his shortcomings behind a plethora of excuses.

No job?

It was because he was a free thinker who refused to be a slave to the system.

No car?

All the tickets he had accumulated caused his license to be suspended; it was just another trap by the system, and he would not dare pay such an unwarranted debt.

No money?

Money was a social construct but getting on food stamps from the government for some food was OK by Seth.

For a while, I was fooled by the masks he wore. Call it naivete, call it loneliness, but whatever the cause, in the beginning Seth hung the moon and stars in my eyes. It took a long time of nearly constant disappointments to chip away the rose-colored tint on my glasses, and by the time I was a few months pregnant with my son, I was completely disillusioned. I didn't know what I wanted my life to look like, but I knew that Seth wasn't even standing in the frame when I pictured my future. My realizations didn't help me when it came to be influencing my situation, however. If anything, seeing how I was falling short and being unable to change it was its own brand of torture.

One day, I parked the taxicab and wandered into the health food store where a good friend of mine named Caroline worked. Ironically, it was the same store where Seth and I had our first date. It was also where he ate religiously and was able to contact a lot of his pothead clients. I was about seven months pregnant and broke as a joke. My daughter was spending more time away from me and more time with her dad. When Caroline asked how I was, I broke down in tears as I confessed to her that I was not doing well at all. She could see that I was depressed and suggested that I attend a personal development program. According to Caroline, people who graduated from the program went on to make positive changes in their lives — changes that included things like going back to school or writing a book. It sounded like exactly *what* I needed, exactly *when* I needed it.

Caroline promised that the program would be good for me, and the introductory class convinced me that she was right. That day we were given a booklet that asked us to compare what our life was like with what we wished it could be. On one hand I was broke, pregnant, and depressed, while on the other I not only wanted to be happy but to be able to fully express myself in all aspects of life, something I'd never been allowed to do. I was shocked when — after reading my results to the other members of the class — I was told that I was a natural. They laughed when I expressed my fear that I was suffering a midlife crisis; since I was only twenty-seven at the time, I can see why, but there was no other way to describe what I was going through. They had no idea of the emotional, verbal, and even physical abuse I had endured over the past four years.

That day was a significant part of my growth because it revealed a road I never would have considered before. It was a whisper of what would one day become a shout. An inkling that would lead me to my place in the grand design. I might not have been having a midlife crisis in the traditional sense, but I *was* in the middle of a metamorphosis. I was beginning to recognize my old habits and belief systems for what they were: dead skin. There was no telling who I would be once I finished washing the old Montrella away, but I was eager to meet her. After only a couple of hours in an introductory class, it was like the floodgates had been opened for me. Once I saw the possibilities there was no turning back, and I threw myself into my journey of self-discovery with an enthusiasm I hadn't felt for a long time. Though I was a lifetime learner, Seth had gotten me to ignore that side of myself for years. In fact, he was not open to any new information, but instead chose to operate on the same old information. He was against anyone who thought differently. He had to be the man and he had to have the final say. The good thing is that he was not around and could not squash my enthusiasm when I got a hold of this new viewpoint. Hallelujah!

I wanted change so badly, I could taste it. Unfortunately, people who say that you can't put a price on happiness have clearly never tried. The program cost over $400.00, and I couldn't fathom how I could get that kind of money together when I was barely scraping by. But, that day, I did something radical; I made the conscious decision that I would figure it out and register for the full course which was a three-and-a-half-day class. I didn't know how I would get the money, but I knew that I would pull it off somehow. There is like a rush of adrenaline when one returns to dreaming again after being around those who do not have any dreams but make sure you do not dare to dream also.

Back home, I got a call from an old high school friend of mine, Bonnie. Assuming this conversation would take the same course as our many other gossipy tones would, I asked her if she'd ever heard of the program and she admitted that she had. She expressed how unhappy she was with their refund process. She said she was fighting to get her money back. She said that her other friend had introduced her to it, and during the excitement, she'd signed up. She had decided it was not for her and she didn't want to take the class. However, their policy was no cash refunds. It could, however, be transferred to another time or to another person. Then the craziest thing happened; she said, nonchalantly, "You can have my ticket."

REFLECTIONS

They say that when one door closes, another opens. It felt as if this door had been waiting for me the entire time. It was around this time that I realized that I was the one who had the power to shape my reality. Once I made the decision and spoke it into existence, everything I needed simply fell into place. It was a blessing waiting for me to accept it with open arms and once I did, all the obstacles I thought would interfere with my success disappeared.

Most people go through life with a miserly mindset. In other words, the glass is half empty rather than half full. They aren't necessarily selfish, but they see the world as not having enough: not enough resources, not enough money, not enough love, not enough avenues for success. If I've learned anything, it's that life lacks nothing. In truth, it is ripe with abundance. Those who don't understand this believe that there isn't enough happiness and prosperity for everyone, so that when someone succeeds, they covet that success. Jealously plays tricks on their minds and sows self-doubt and even bitterness. These feelings have a way of feeding into the belief that we each only receive what we deserve; if we end up with a no-good man, a small part of us is convinced that it's because we deserve him. If we aren't happy at our jobs, it's because we think it's as good as we'll ever get so we might as well make the most of it.

It's easier sometimes to think that the bad that comes our way is a by-product of something fundamentally flawed within us rather than a choice. I use the word "choice" because by not proactively deciding that you want more for yourself, you aren't really living life so much as reacting to it. It was also about taking responsibility for my life and my destiny. Once I decided to better my situation and stopped making excuses for Seth, everything fell into place. It was like watching a child fit toy blocks into their corresponding shapes. For years I'd been trying to shove a square into a circle and crying foul when things refused to line up. Shifting my focus and widening my perception allowed the change I'd been hoping for year after year to come into fruition in a matter of weeks.

It was proof that God's gifts truly are boundless. He stands waiting, arms laden with blessings upon blessings. The majority will waste their lives sitting before him, pouting over what the next child got. Others will clutch at pieces of coal and call it gold. For those of us who not only see the gifts awaiting us but are willing to receive them, there exists a world of possibility.

For those who are ready to take that step, it's important to realize that in order to receive the blessings you have coming, you must first make room for them in your life and in your spirit. But we'll delve into that lesson more deeply in a later chapter.

I've always been the type of person who believed in paying things forward, and I wanted to teach the people I loved about what I'd learned during my time in the program. The class changed my entire life and I didn't hesitate to tell everyone that I knew about it. Seth, of course, was unimpressed. He felt that I was "sacrificing my seed" and that my refusing to marry him just because I was pregnant was my ultimate betrayal. Whenever I talked about the program, he regarded me with disdain and made snide comments about how I'd been brainwashed. He was visiting Florida for a while before I started the classes and by the time he came back, I was a completely different person. He was disappointed to learn that I had put a full stop to the dysfunctional cycle we had been going through for years whereby he was in and out of my life. It wasn't just in his imagination either. I *felt* different: emotionally, physically, mentally, and spiritually. I was at a crossroads within myself, stuck between the past and the future. The class had reawakened my old sense of values and had helped me remember just how important my faith had always been, and still was, to me. I knew that in order to create a future in which I was fully self-expressed, I would need to once again embrace the beliefs that had once been my bedrock. The same beliefs that Seth had done such a thorough job of undermining. But also, the same beliefs that helped me overcome so many milestones to date, including poverty, my mom's drug addiction, teenage pregnancy, and rape.

It was more evident than ever before that if I had any hope of moving forward, I needed to cut Seth loose. I was fed up with him and his negativity, and one day I put aside everything that was holding me back and took scissors to all his clothes. Cutting up his belongings felt good. It was my way of taking my power back, of proving to the both of us that his rules would no longer be allowed to dictate my life. Seth had always been a materialistic man. He took pride in the trinkets he owned. I sometimes wondered if he'd ever really cared about me or if I was just one more possession for him to polish and place upon a shelf. Something to prove his prowess to himself and everyone that saw me. In many ways, Seth was constantly searching for his own sense of self-worth, despite his outwardly cocky demeanor. He found value in the material, the shallow, and he was always afraid to dig any deeper or push himself to the next level because he knew that he lacked the substance that most people believed to be built into their DNA. Whatever the truth, destroying his clothes did the trick, and after a heated argument Seth gathered what little he had left and walked out of my life for good.

~ Make no more excuses—take your power back! ~

Chapter 5: *The Sewing Kit*

WHAT HOLDS IT ALL TOGETHER

> *Faith is the only known antidote for failure!*
> *—Napoleon Hill*

Thanks to everything he'd put me through, being with Seth taught me a lot about myself. Our relationship proved that faith is just as important as values. Thus, every time you reach in your purse be reminded that the sewing kit in it stands for your faith. Regardless of what you believe, it's imperative that you believe in something so that you don't fall for anything. My faith is what shaped my values; it was the standard for my morality and the bar by which I measured the rest of the world. I sacrificed my relationship with family and friends to be with Seth. My loyalty to him and his "knowledge" led me from the church. Rather than holding on to my faith, I'd allowed him to convince me that he deserved my devotion more than God did. This man took the place of the divine source, and my values were reshaped accordingly. I'd placed all my trust into this one person, confident that he was somehow infallible because he'd said all the right things at just the right time.

It was like building your home out of straw instead of brick. It was no wonder the slightest breeze had the power to bring it all crashing down. With Seth gone, I was able to concentrate on re-building myself from the ground up. I went back to basics and delved into topics that stimulated my mind and my imagination. Rather than allow my pregnancy to be an experience that was happening to me, I educated myself and took classes so that this second birth would in no way resemble the first. I was used to being dismissed and mistreated and if I wanted things to change then I had to demand better not only from myself but from others. The first step to accomplishing that began with learning about how things *should* work so that I would have the knowledge and courage to call people out when they deviated from that.

It's the same with life.

You have to establish a foundation, a standard, that you can measure all of your actions by. Without it, you're signing yourself up for failure. Imagine a rocket shooting towards space. There are set coordinates designed to help it achieve success. But what would happen if you kept entering different coordinates or the wrong ones? Not only would you miss your goal entirely, but you also run the risk of spiraling out of control. While it might seem easy to deviate from what you believe in, never forget that your faith and spirituality are the coordinates by which you set your life. The more code that you add, subtract, or switch out entirely, the more obscure your path becomes. Do it enough and you'll end up flying aimlessly and if you're not careful, you'll eventually crash and burn.

I'm not here to tell you what to believe. What I am here to do is to tell you that belief in something, regardless of the form that belief takes, is tantamount to success. It is important to first acknowledge—and then to honor—yourself as a spiritual being. Faith is what holds us accountable when we go against our own moral compass. It's the north star that we follow to find ourselves once again. Faith also helps us distinguish between which values are important and which ones we can leave by the wayside. For instance, Seth preached about what I should and shouldn't be doing often. But, because I had my own faith to compare his teachings to, I was able to distinguish what was the result of his ego. Without that standard to go by, I might have been too far under his spell to ever pull myself out again.

As it was, Seth and I separated when I was around six months pregnant. Plenty of time for me to plan how I wanted my baby to come into the world. My second childbirth was a home birth, the culmination of everything I'd learned about myself and the way I deserved to be treated. No one was berating me while I was pushing him into the world, and there was no shadow of violence to dim the joy of meeting him for the first time. On the contrary, one of the three midwives who tended to my son's birth said, "This is the most peaceful birth I have ever attended." I must admit that I kind of overdosed on watching Japanese women give natural births so harmoniously. The connection between us was just as strong and just as instantaneous as what I had experienced with my firstborn. Looking into those brown eyes and feeling his small hand in mine somehow made the years before it seemed paltry. Everything I'd gone through with Seth was worth it when I finally held the fruit of my labors in my arms and heard his sweet cry for the first time.

I knew that I was blessed because without meeting Seth and staying with him for so long I never would have brought my king of a son into this world. Even worse, I never would have known that he was missing from my life, though I'm sure I would have continued to search for something to fill the void he seemed to assuage by simply breathing. If only every life lesson could end just as sweetly. Though, perhaps they can once more of us realize what we're searching for.

Everyone goes through life trying to fill an emptiness inside, hoping to find their reason for being. Some choose to ease the ache with alcohol, or drugs, or sex. Some search for the cure in the arms of other people, only to end up hurt and confused when that void is still just as deep as before. At the end of the day, it takes faith to have purpose. The two go hand in hand and it's impossible to fully understand one without the other. Even an atheist must have faith in him- or herself. For those of us who crave the comfort of a higher power, our faith in the divine is what gives us strength.

The problem with placing your faith in other people is that human beings, by definition and reputation, are fallible. We each have faults and doubts and are limited by our own limitations even in our thinking. We've all fallen prey to pride and are prone to acts of pettiness. None of us are perfect, and while it's OK not to be, it isn't OK to build your life around something that is inherently flawed. Let's look at the rocket I mentioned earlier; would you rather build it out of clay and dirt or steel? Not only do you need to maintain a steady course in order to reach your goals, you also need to ensure that you have all the tools necessary to get where you're trying to go.

When you lack the proper materials, you're constantly searching for something (or someone) to patch the holes and cracks that appear over the course of your journey, understanding all too well that it's only a matter of time before everything you've built comes crashing down. My faith is the glue that held my craft together, my religion is the coordinates by which I steer my life. Without the two, I would never get off the ground and my life would be spent staring up at the stars instead of flying amongst them.

It's a fine line to walk, to become the person you want to be so that you can find the love that you deserve. In order to succeed you must put in the work and sometimes that means pausing long enough to remember what's really important. Faith can help us do that, which is why it's the perfect addition to any woman's purse. Faith is our needle and thread. It is the tool we use to patch up the rips and tears we find over the course of our journey. Without it, tears can become gaping holes. Plus, the items that you so carefully chose to go into your purse are now at risk of slipping away. How can you expect anyone else to help fulfill your spirit when you're falling apart at the seams? When you lose your values at every relationship encounter, and when every new lesson learned is just seconds away from being discarded?? It would be like trying to fill a cracked cup with water. It doesn't matter whether it's half empty or half full if it's too broken to be of any use.

You see, Seth worked hard to fill me with fear and deny my soul. He spent countless hours trying to convince me that all pastors were nothing but criminals with a whole lot of pride whose only job was to con people like me into consistently paying their tithes. Of course, this is not true. That fool didn't realize my spiritual journey and how I was destined to return to it. What he didn't know was that when I was only thirteen years old, I was recognized by my beloved pastor, requested to serve like a minister praying behind the pastor as he delivered his sermon. Had I kept that up, I would likely have become a preacher! Can I get an amen? As church folks always say, "That devil is a liar!"

This chapter has been full of metaphors, but it's nearly impossible to discuss such an intangible concept like "faith" without giving you something concrete to draw from. Some people don't understand what faith is because they're so used to giving it to the wrong thing that their understanding of it has been corrupted. The target of your faith should help you grow as a person. It should reflect an ideal greater than your physical self and its limitations so that you have something to aspire to. Having faith isn't easy, but the cool thing about it is that the more you put it through, the stronger it becomes and with it on your side, there's no way that you can lose. I work with numerous couples who can attest to the fact that their faith served a major role in saving their marriage during times of discord. For any healthy and romantic relationship, you want to incorporate faith practices. If you start dating someone, no matter how attractive they may seem, if they are pulling you away from your spiritual routine—whether that be going to your church, synagogue, mosque, temple, Kingdom Hall, yoga studio, prayer room, or meditation mat—RUN!

RECIPE #2 - The Prodigal Sun Burger

When it comes to finding your way back to your spiritual values, it's essential to choose the right components to help you stay on the right track. The Prodigal Sun is a collection of ingredients that everyone has at their disposal, and it's quick and easy to make. This dish is perfect for every occasion and sure to please even the most discerning palate.

Prep Time: Varies   Serving Size: 1

Directions:
1. Write down the current state of your life.
2. What are your dreams? Your short-term goals? Write them down and place them somewhere visible so that you can look at them every day.
3. Compare each list; what steps do you need to take to make the changes you're seeking?
4. Consider what it is you believe in. Where do these beliefs stem from? How have they helped you grow as a person?
5. Look at your last relationship. What have you had to sacrifice for the sake of the other person? Were these sacrifices positive or did you lose the best parts of yourself?
6. Acknowledge why you gave up these things and what doing so accomplished. It's important to understand what you were willing to trade your values for since this will give you an idea of what it is you feel you're missing.

7. Remember the moments when faith in something helped sustain you. How did you feel at that time? What part did your faith play in the decisions you made?
8. Realize that anyone who makes you give up your faith is probably not the right person for you.
9. Accept the fact that the foundation you fall back on is directly affected by the beliefs you hold.

Additional Notes (Repeat daily or as often as needed. Can be used individually for some much-needed nourishment between meals.):

"Loving myself allows me to better love others.

~ I am respected and admired by others for being so faithful

~ I am wealthy spiritually, financially, and physically

~ I am surrounded by spiritually healthy and loving people"

Nutritional Facts - Per Serving
- 40% Self-love
- 40% Acceptance
- 20% Ownership of your own life

10/10 - Would Recommend

~ Stay on the right track as you learn to love yourself and others. ~

Chapter 6: *Badr & Asad*

For the second time in my life, I found myself facing the hardships of motherhood alone. Unlike with my firstborn, being a single mother after my son was born was a decision that I made for myself. It wasn't forced upon me by circumstances and cruelty. It was a mark of just how much I'd grown as a woman over the last ten years that I *chose* to step out into the world on my own. Many women, too many, stay in toxic relationships because they're familiar. They don't know anything else and the unknown might be worse than what they're leaving behind. Uncharted territory is not a path many would walk, especially with children to think about.

This new, bolder, wiser Montrella was ready to take on the world. After I cut ties with Seth, it was like a physical weight had been lifted off my shoulders. The future was brighter and ripe with possibility. I knew what I wanted, and I was confident that I'd figure out how to get it. If being with Seth had taught me anything, it was that I wanted more for myself and my children. While I left before the damage he could inflict was permanently engraved, the years we'd spent with him had wrought changes within each of us.

After our son was born, Seth was there; or rather, he was in and out in his usually inconsistent way of doing things. While my son never saw his parents in a relationship together, we were both very much a part of his early life. Thanks, in part, to my belief that a man should be involved with his kids. Like Reggie, I was always willing to put my personal grievances aside so that my son could get to know his father. Was it naivete on my part to think that Seth could be a better parent than he had a partner? Maybe it was a misplaced sense of obligation. Whatever the case, it wasn't long before I began to regret giving him the opportunity to prove me wrong yet again.

I had been adamant about giving my son a fair chance at this thing called life, without being solely influenced by Seth's irrational beliefs and craziness as my daughter had been. I told myself that limited visitation would be enough to mitigate anything Seth threw his way. It wasn't until my son broke his hip that I realized that I would need to take more drastic measures. The diet that Seth had forced upon us all was nutrient deficient. When our baby boy broke his hip, it took him almost twice as long to heal because Seth wasn't feeding him properly. He was still stuck in the same mindset he'd been in when we'd been together; the same mindset that had helped drive my daughter away and into Reggie's waiting arms.

It's worth noting that while this wasn't the only thing Seth had done that made me question his ability to be a good father, it was the most eye opening. With that one act of consistent and deliberate negligence, Seth showed me that his mercurial ideals were more important than the health and well-being of our child. He'd shown me just how far he was willing to go, just how blinded he was willing to be, to maintain this persona that he'd built out of the ashes of his dismantled beliefs.

It was hard to admit to myself at the time, but even though I was no longer with Seth, he still had somewhat of an influence on part of my heart. We'd been together for so long, and regardless of our disagreements he had been there as a father figure to my daughter when even her own father shied away from the responsibility. Prior to my son, life would have been easier if I could have hated him, but as it was it was hard to turn off my feelings. My love for him had kept me going back to him repeatedly knowing full well that he was selling weed. It had kept me going back even after he put hands on me. It kept me there despite all the times he left my bed so that he could slink into another's.

For years, love kept me trapped in a relationship that was slowly eating away at me, and if it hadn't been for Khalid and China, I wasn't sure if I would have had the wherewithal to pull myself out of it. Maybe that was why it was so hard to accept his carelessness when it came to the health of our son. I wasn't just angry after I'd found out what was going on, I was hurt. He'd managed to prove that the same things that had come between us would always be there. There was no changing someone that was set in his ways, and it took me a while to accept that I couldn't remain stagnant with him, not even in my heart.

After our son's healing was directly affected by Seth's asinine diet, I took him to court. The judge ruled in my favor and Seth lost custody. On paper, I was free, once and for all, to raise my son the way that I knew he deserved. There was so much that I did with my second child that I wished I could have done with my first. But things happen when they are meant to. The woman I used to be would not have been able to afford private school for her kids for one. For another, I appreciated my hard-won sense of independence so much more than I had before it had been snatched from me. There was so much of my life that changed for the better after I left Seth. Not just on an emotional and mental level, but from a financial aspect as well.

While we were still together, I struggled to make opportunities for all of us, but Seth made it nearly impossible. Even so, I somehow convinced Seth to take a class with me. We were unhappy at home and I was tired of fighting all the time. At the time I was pregnant with my son and I thought a parenting class would be good for us, not just for the sake of my daughter but for my newborn's as well. All our classmates had been ordered to take the course by the courts in order to keep their kids. At first, I thought that the teacher's interest in me had to do with the fact that Seth and I were the only volunteers in the group. The woman teaching the class was getting her master's in social work and during our last week, her supervisor came to watch our presentations.

For my presentation, I chose to discuss how black children possessed untapped genius. To my surprise, the parent educator and her supervisor were both extremely impressed by what I had to say, and afterwards I was asked if I had an interest in social work because I was a natural. I was offered a position as a parent educator despite my lack of degree. The experience was so amazingly validating. Seth was always putting me down and making me feel worthless and stupid, so to have someone believe in me and my capabilities was a big deal. The job itself was a gift from God, but just as life changing was my newfound sense of worth. It all proved Seth's words as the vicious lies that they were.

Thanks to my teacher, my self-confidence got a major boost. As someone who loved to learn, the position seemed as if it had been made for me. I'd been ready for a change in my life, and when it came to me the sense of emotional upliftment that filled me left me giddy and hopeful for the future for the first time in a long time.

That moment set me on the path back to finding myself after being lost for so long with Seth. Not only did it help advance my life, it also cleared the way for me to remember my values. Before taking the job, my understanding of social work had been limited. What I learned there ignited my passion for learning and finally helped me break free of the cycle I'd fallen into of allowing myself to get pulled into Seth's orbit of toxicity. A social worker is born, not made, and finding my path put all my other setbacks in a new perspective.

Before social work and before Seth, I'd attempted college twice only to drop out because I had no clear idea what I wanted to be, let alone study. It left me feeling like a wanderer and a failure, just further proof at the time that I was "inadequate", and all the things Seth told me were true. Though he did his best to break me down, I don't regret the role he played in my life. If not for Seth and what he put me through, I never would have stumbled onto a defined path and figured out my purpose. More than anything else, I would not have given birth to my son, the bringer of happiness.

Once I had a goal to work towards, I was determined to achieve it and more focused than ever before. That goal was to give my little king the best life that any mother could offer. With a new mindset and Seth out of the picture, the pieces finally came together. I was lucky because there were people in my life who not only inspired me, but who saw my potential. The personal development course was only the tip of the iceberg when it came to me realizing just how much I was capable of, however. What I discovered was that there was so much that I had always had the potential to see through, I just had to allow myself the chance to explore my own capabilities. Society teaches women, especially black women, to diminish themselves in thousands of different ways. Once I gave myself permission to flourish, everything simply fell into place, almost as if it had been waiting for me.

True freedom is when you dare to start living your wildest dreams, and after Seth and I broke up I went back to college, laser focused on finally earning my degree in honor of my new baby. Against nearly an entire community's worth of encouragement, I did not choose the local, inexpensive university I could have gone to for free. Instead I chose a Catholic school program that opened even more doors for me. In 2004, I distinctly remember holding my youngest up on one hip with the help of my African-print baby wrap that formed a perfectly fitted pouch for him. I also remember all my white privileged classmates and professors staring at me like I was not only the "Black" student, but crazy as well. Reflecting on it, I was quite bold. Hey, that is what a mother must do sometimes to change her black son's life trajectory. Till this day, one of my biggest—and most challenging—accomplishments was earning my first degree in interdisciplinary studies and social work from the Catholic University of America (CUA). The only black person at the school, I was always painfully aware of how different I was from my peers. I came from a lower socioeconomic bracket, not to mention I had to attend classes with a newborn in tow. But I started to appreciate all the wisdom I had gained over the years. Real life had prepared me to do well in school despite the odds stacked against me. I was also able to get creative and explore different experiences: experiences that I had only yearned for up until that point. I made it my business to study things that genuinely interested me, and this made all the difference. I used social issues, real-life examples, books and movies that helped portray my story in my research, papers, and presentations in the classroom. At last I had a clear path and could finally see the light at the end of the long tunnel. It all was starting to make sense and I could see how everything was linked to everything.

One of my dreams has always been to go to the motherland. I decided that my classroom experience would expand outside of the classroom and across distant seas. So yummy! Not surprisingly, Catholic University had a great study abroad program, though it was only to Europe and a few "safe" spots in Latin America. During my sophomore year, I used my natural resourcefulness to identify a program to finally go to the motherland while still receiving credits that I could transfer to CUA. Through the University of Nevada Las Vegas's University Studies Abroad Consortium (USAC) I spent the summer in Ghana where I met my mentor. It was a strange juxtaposition. From the beginning Seth had always been eager to put me in my place—which, according to him, was beneath him. He always had to be the smartest, the strongest, and the most cultured. Seth always talked about Africa and how we were the original descendants of Africans, but then that fool was too afraid to get on a plane. He said he would go to Africa on a boat one day. What a joke! The closest he ever got to Africa was in my apartment in DC during my son's African naming ceremony. That's how much of a hypocrite he was. He was a man full of fear, and the moment I stepped off that plane I knew that I had fulfilled something no one, especially him, would have thought me capable of.

I traveled a lot after that, glorying in the chance to show my children a world outside of DC. During a trip to Honduras with my son, we followed a world-famous herbalist for over a month. There my son was a fresh thirty days young. I hiked with him and went to hot springs with him. It was full of nature, beauty, and calmness. As my son sucked on my breast for his nutrition, I placed us both in an environment that was spiritually and mentally uplifting.

I'd been beneath a man's thumb for so long that I wanted to live. I wanted to shed the fear and doubt and worry that seemed to be a mother's constant companion so that I could give my children the role model I wished I'd had when I was growing up.

But, like all journeys that matter, mine had its ups and downs.

One of the bumps in the road was named Asad.

Dancing was like therapy for me and I'd always loved reggae music. So, when I passed my finals for the first semester of my junior year at Catholic, I made a beeline for the dance floor to celebrate. There was a lot on my plate at that point in my life. So much so that it was easy to forget that I was still young. A night out away from the kids where I could go and forget myself in the rhythm of the music and the energy of the crowd would give me a much-needed pick-me-up to get through the rest of the week.

I was convinced that men were just a distraction, and I was on a mission to get back in the good graces with life. Which was why, when I met Asad that night, I already knew that his efforts to impress me would fall on deaf ears. I'd seen him around before. That wasn't my first time at the club and each time I was there he made an effort to catch my eye. I'd even seen him dancing with Caitlin once, which led me to believe that the two might have known one another.

As I'd done countless times before, I ignored him and focused on the task at hand. I was happy to finally find a dance partner and eager to release some of the pent-up stress that had been plaguing me since the beginning of finals. I tried to avoid him, but Asad was nothing if not persistent. Everywhere I turned he was there, offering me a drink and trying to strike up a conversation. Eventually the two of us ended up on the dance floor together. He kept insisting on buying me a drink as if he didn't believe that I didn't do alcohol. As it turned out, he was Muslim and wasn't a drinker either. In the end, he got me a bottle of water to quench my thirst. I appreciated the gesture since I'd been sweating from all the winding and grinding instigated by the dancehall tunes of Buju Banton, Bounty Killer, and Beenie Man.

I would have been content if that had been the extent of the night. Feeling beautiful and desired, riding the wave of relief and exaltation from succeeding when I'd thought I'd fail, and simply enjoying myself for what seemed like the first time in a long time. Love wasn't on my radar, and even if it had been Asad wouldn't have been my first choice. He was tall and slim, and you could just tell that he was a hardworking man from his demeanor. He seemed perfect...I just never found him attractive. I hadn't expected to get along so well with him that night, but once I made the decision to do so he was surprisingly easy to talk to. While it had been fun joking and dancing with him, it didn't change the fact that he wasn't my type. So, when the party wound down and he asked for my number, I politely declined.

"There's no point," I told him honestly. "I'm leaving soon to study abroad in Morocco." Yep, I was proud to soon be setting out for my second study abroad trip in college. This time during my junior year and through another great program that I'd found! Rather than discouraging him with my travel declaration, Asad's brows shot up as if he were even more intrigued. I learned later that men really love when a woman exhibits a certain amount of mystique as I was. I got that curiosity a lot from men. There was always a sense of satisfaction when I admitted just how blessed I was. It was almost as if I were still battling that little girl, I'd been the ugly one, the teen mother, the dead end.

Personal sense of accomplishment aside, I was excited about taking my daughter on this trip with me. My son would be staying with my aunt in New York until we got back to the States. Our lives had been topsy-turvy lately, and I wanted to spend some quality time with my growing young lady and reconnect with her. The men in our lives had worked a number on us both and between Reggie and Seth both trying to turn her against me, the two of us were having a hard time reaching one another. She was also still adjusting to having to share her mother with her new brother, and I was hoping this shared experience would bring her back to me.

Which was just one more reason why I wasn't looking to start a relationship. My kids and I had been through enough in that department and I was leery about introducing yet another factor into our lives when we were just hitting our stride. Not that Asad wasn't a sweet man. He was simply intense and persistent. More so than anyone else that I was used to. It was as if once he made up his mind to be with me, there was nothing I could do or say to convince him otherwise. It would have raised all sorts of red flags if he wasn't such a nice guy. Everything he did, he did in earnest, as if crossing oceans and scaling mountains for your woman was just par for the course.

"That's alright," he assured me. "I don't mind putting in a little work."

I didn't realize it at the time, but his casual dismissal of the fact that there would soon be a literal ocean between us wasn't just posturing. He'd meant it. From that day forward, we talked almost every day while I was abroad either over the phone or via Skype video chat.

He looked at me as if I hung the sun, moon, and stars and after being put down by Seth for so long, Asad's reaction to me was a breath of fresh air. His reaction to me was an assurance: "*I still got it!*" Though I made it clear over the course of our relationship that things wouldn't progress the way he so clearly wanted them to, nothing deterred him. Asad seemed to have plenty of disposable income and wasn't shy about spending it on yours truly. Every time I turned around, he was showering me or the kids with gifts and taking me on trips.

On the surface, we worked.

Here was a man who was not only open-minded, he also treated me with respect and kindness. Since he was from Africa, he had an international mindset that was perfect for someone like me who was finally embracing my desire to see the world. He listened to me and it seemed like he valued what I had to say. He was the perfect friend.

But when it came to romance . . .there was nothing there...no sparks to the flame. Can someone please pass me a light?

He was a good man...he just wasn't the *right* one. Don't get me wrong, the attention was flattering, and it was nice to be around a man who seemed so attentive and understanding. But I didn't want him to feel as if I owed him anything. There are men who feel as if every kindness is a deposit that they can cash out later in the form of sex. Asad didn't seem like that type of person, but I'd been misled before and I was unwilling to put myself into a situation I would have to maneuver out of later. The two of us were never intimate because I was content to keep our relationship platonic. A situation that Asad was apparently happy to go along with.

What made the situation even more awkward was the fact that my family loved him. I was constantly getting bombarded with reasons why the two of us should be together and what a catch he was. I knew that the reason they all seemed so eager to have him as part of the family was because he had money. He wasn't just happy to spend money on me either; in fact, he was quick to treat my relatives to birthday dinners and holiday gifts as well. Being with Asad was contrary to my own desires, but eventually the encouragement from every side wore me down and my protests petered off to nothing.

This is where I must pause. After all, I can't talk about my relationship with Asad and how things eventually spiraled out of control with us, without also talking about Badr. The other hurdle in my life. The two of us met before the birth of my son, when Seth and I were still together. Back then I used to attend a few of the Afrocentric meetings at Howard University. The meetings were led by an Afrocentrist who spoke passionately about the origins and injustices of white supremacist culture. One of the women I'd met during these talks introduced me to Badr after seeing me with my daughter and deciding that I needed a man in my life. Her words struck a chord within me but probably not for the reasons she would have wanted. Seth and I were going through one of our "off" phases and she simply reminded me of what I was already going through.

When I first laid eyes on Badr it was like a gentle hand reached inside of me and lovingly touched my heart and soul at the same time. He appeared at the hotel that I was working at with flowers in hand, glistening dark, flawless skin and a dazzling smile that revealed teeth whiter than any toothpaste commercial I had ever seen. He was my kind of gorgeous.

A woman I had become acquainted with while my daughter and I attended the late Dr. Frances Cress Welsing's lectures at the Blackburn Center of Howard University was always telling me how she thought I needed a man, and one day she decided to put her money where her mouth was. She went on and on about this friend she had who was just so wonderful (Badr). She said that he was not here now, but that he would be coming from Africa soon and she really wanted us to meet.

For our first date we grabbed a bite to eat after I got off work and then went to a dance club. Not only did he look good, Badr was one of the best dancers amongst any guys I had ever dated. But Badr's timing could not have been worse. After Seth, I told myself that I'd had my fill of no-good men. He'd cheated on me and emotionally abused me enough to last a lifetime, and I just knew that I was finally wise enough and mature enough to know better, to be able to tell the Dogs from the Prince Charmings. Not that I was actively looking for love. A part of me believed that I would never be as attracted to another man as I was when I first met Seth.

The two of us went out on a date, but my mind and heart were still so wrapped up in Seth that Badr stood little chance of holding my attention for long. We had our first date in the same club where I would eventually meet Asad. Not only was Badr handsome with his dark brown skin and thick African accent, he was also an amazing dancer. A part of my brain wanted to dismiss him and agonize over what Seth was doing and who he was sleeping with this time, but instead, my eyes drifted shut as I moved. For a moment I let myself ignore the crush of people and simply allowed the music to take over. For someone who grew up as a wallflower, the dance floor was one of the few places where I felt comfortable enough to lower my defenses. I danced like no one was watching because in my mind it didn't matter if they were. I did enjoy the looks of admiration Badr sent my way that night as I sauntered past in heels and a dress that fit just right, winding like a snake charmer while the reggae music swept over us both. My hips were a call to action and Badr was eager to answer, leading every step of the way.

The night had been ripe with possibilities, but in the end, I'd gone right back to Seth instead of pursuing what could have been. I didn't mind because as much as I was attracted to Badr, if I'd taken that path all those years ago, I never would have had my son. Like I say, things meant to happen in our lives have a season. Badr and I got our second chance, though there was no way I could have predicted just how much being with him would change my life.

If you've ever read a fairy tale or watched a Disney movie, you know the magical allure of Prince Charming. He's dashing, perfect; he's the man who swoops in to save you from heartbreak and struggle. An epitome of manliness that isn't rooted in selfishness and dishonesty. Growing up, I'd had little time for a make-believe Casanova. It's hard to imagine Prince Eric walking through the ghetto in search of someone like me, and any glass slippers that found their way into *my* neighborhood were likely to end up on stage somewhere surrounded by dollar bills and poles drenched with sweat. Before I was old enough to begin asking myself what I *did* want in a man, Reggie was there to snuff out my light. All in all, I never gave much thought to what I considered the "perfect man" because I never gave much thought as to how *I* wanted to be treated. I guess I thought of it like a fast-food restaurant and that men come ready-made to order.

People forget that knowing how you want to be loved is an essential part in deciding what you want from a partner. Thanks to Seth and Reggie, I knew what I *didn't* want, but that was about it. So, when Badr and I finally reconnected after several long years apart, I was blown away by the connection between us. He was nothing like Asad. While the two men were equally persistent, Badr left me feeling as if I'd been romanced whereas Asad simply wore away at my defenses until I gave him what he was searching for.

Badr was everything I never knew that I wanted. He treated me with respect and listened to what I had to say without being condescending. We could talk and laugh with one another. He was the kind of partner who I knew would always be there when I needed him the most. Badr was dependable, reliable, and affectionate. By the way he danced, I just assumed that he was also an amazing lover. In a perfect world, after he and I began dating again it would have been curtains closed. Our wedding should have been my first and last and Badr should have been my everything. But the lessons I learned from him were just as much about the mask I fell in love with as they were the secrets, he kept hidden beneath it.

We were married in a mosque.

When I thought of marriage at all, I imagined a ceremony that was more traditional and in league with my Christian upbringing. In my mind's eye I was in a wedding dress and surrounded by the people I loved. My daughter was the flower girl while my son acted as a ring bearer. My father would walk me down the aisle, and for a moment life would be a little sweeter. A day that was all mine, that would make all the heartache that came before it worth it in a way that nothing else could have.

The reality was quite different. I told myself that when you loved someone, then compromise was an inevitable part of making a relationship work. The problem is that when you're the only person compromising, it's no longer a compromise but a sacrifice. Badr's brand of love was particularly demanding. He had a way of making me forget all the little ways that I was ignoring my better judgment. A way of making even the most outrageous suggestion seem as if it made sense. There were so many times that I raised my concerns to Badr and each time he talked me back down. It left me feeling as if I were overreacting or simply seeing an issue in the wrong light. All considered, it kept me questioning myself. A situation I'd promised to never find myself in again. It was harder to break the habit than I'd thought it would be. What made it even more difficult was the fact that I didn't even realize when I was doing it. In the heat of the moment, giving in felt less like being manipulated and more like making the most practical decision.

In the end, it all translated into one thing. My wedding wasn't anything like what I'd hoped for in my heart of hearts. He had no family there to support him and neither did I. Without those familiar faces the mosque was cold, dark, and impersonal, so much so that I couldn't shake the feeling that I was unwelcome there. Despite my misgivings and discomfort, I exchanged vows with Badr with no one there to celebrate my nuptials or give me away. On the surface I was happy, but there was an undercurrent of disappointment and shame. The ceremony itself was cheapened by the lack of family and proper tradition. Aside from that, I was not even Muslim. I knew that just as surely as I knew my own name. There was so much about that day that was simply wrong, though I did my best to shove my doubts aside and simply enjoy my wedding for what it was.

My wedding didn't have to be perfect, but I would have been content if the day was one that I could hold special in my heart. Something that was nearly impossible to do when I had little to no say in the proceedings. In fact, it's hard now to even consider the ceremony itself a wedding, for a number of reasons.

For one, we were married on April Fool's Day. Badr paid a $100.00 dowry for the honor of taking my hand. At the time I didn't think much of the exchange—more concerned with understanding the custom itself than the price. I was really taken aback when the imam asked what I thought would be a good amount and it was the first thing that popped out of my mouth, almost as a joke. It wasn't until later that I learned how paltry my dowry price was. Many grooms paid the family of the bride thousands of dollars or exchanged something of great value to cover the cost of a dowry. It was a sign of how much, or how little, the groom considered his new wife to be worth. In many ways, a dowry is a sign of respect and prestige. In Badr's eyes our union was worth less than a utility bill. In hindsight, I'm not sure why I didn't question what was happening more. I was happy, I suppose. Happier than I'd ever been in my previous relationships. Connected spiritually and emotionally with a man that understood and appreciated me. It should have been the perfect recipe for contentment; after all, isn't that what most people spend their entire lives searching for in a partner?

No relationship was perfect.

But how many times would I have to tell myself that before it stopped sounding like an empty platitude? How many times would I have to say it before I no longer had to? No relationship was perfect, and as much as I would have liked Badr and me to be the exception to that, the words rang all too true. For one, Badr was Muslim while I was Christian. Some couples can handle a relationship where their partner doesn't share the same religion, but Badr's beliefs undermined many of my core truths. There were fundamental concepts that the two of us simply couldn't see eye to eye on and it's hard to say now how much of it had to do with religion and how much was a personal choice of his. I also realized as I become more and more spiritually awakened that while many of the core tenets of different religions are the same, people's interpretation of them are as different as an elephant is to a shoe.

The day I was married was supposed to be a culmination of what I'd learned from every failed relationship, from every hurtful word and crushing disappointment. It should have been the product of years of growth, a mindset shaped by the ache of heartbreak, and the awe that comes from having finally seen the world beyond the one you grew up in. I thought I was ready, and with the right man maybe I would have been. Maybe the growth I'd gone through at that point would have been enough to prepare me for something truly worthwhile. As it was, not only did I literally and figuratively sell myself short, I did so, and knew full well that there were red flags with Badr that I'd been all too willing to overlook.

To be up front, the red flags that were raised with Asad were no less numerous than those I'd picked up from Badr. Both men had their issues, though those issues were just as different as Badr and Asad themselves. While Badr and Asad were both Muslims, as far as I could determine they practiced their religion in very different ways. In Badr's case, his way of life jump-started an entirely new set of problems and insecurities. Not because I've ever had an issue with other religions but because I was letting go of my own values—in this case Christianity—for the sake of someone else's needs and wants.

Again.

Badr was proof that yet again, I was all too willing to abandon my spiritual beliefs for the sake of a man-made version of happiness. I knew how dangerous this path was thanks to Seth; I knew from personal experience just how much it would hurt when everything fell apart and I was forced to find myself again, but it was already too late. I'd compromised my foundation under the naïve belief that doing so was somehow helping me grow. The issues between Badr and me went beyond the obvious. These were no petty, shallow concerns. For instance, he liked to flirt. Since he worked as a mechanic and business owner, he met a lot of women, many of whom were single, looking, and as attracted to him as I had been at first sight. Badr was also very, very charismatic. Before and even after our marriage, a friend of his hinted to me about Badr and his extracurricular activities—he was constantly trying to get under every skirt that he bore witness to. But I brushed his warnings aside. While Badr considered polygamy as a staple of his culture, I believed him when he assured me that he wouldn't make moves on the romantic front without talking to me first. I believed him when he told me that I was his first, his main, his only. I believed a lot of things Badr told me.

Why?

Because I loved him.

Not just the thought of him, but the man himself. I loved his charm and wit, his sexuality and confidence. Most of all I loved the way he made me feel when we were together. I could be myself without hesitation or apology. It was like taking a deep breath for the first time since before my assault. It's amazing what someone will put up with for an illusion of acceptance. For the sake of finding somewhere and someone to belong to. I knew what it was to do without and Badr's occasional flirtations were a small price to pay by comparison.

When I first raised my concerns about his lifestyle, he'd explained polygamy to me in great depth. Even going so far as to point out how practical it was to practice such a way of life in a place like Africa where finding a significant other was difficult and marriage was a way to protect an otherwise vulnerable woman. When he spoke, it made sense and I felt selfish and a little silly about asking him to change who he was for the sake of my westernized sensibilities. Seth may have been full of it, but he'd opened my eyes to a lot of things. There was an antiquated way of thinking in America, a conceited way of seeing the world that dismissed any way of life that wasn't considered "American" enough. I prided myself on having an open mind, a student's mind, and the idea of villainizing Badr for his cultural differences didn't sit well with me.

Except, it was one thing to be accepting when the reality of that way of life wasn't at my doorstep. Just because I understood didn't mean that it was something that I wanted for myself or my kids. But, for the sake of our relationship, I was resolved to seeing things through. I reasoned that it wasn't as if polygamy was cheating. After all, Seth had introduced me to other polygamous families who seemed to be doing quite well. Beyond that, men flirted. It was just what they did. There was so much good in our relationship that it seemed petty to make a big deal out of something that I'd come to see as just another normal part of dating.

I don't want to make excuses about the decisions I made during this time in my life. In all honesty, I still had so much growing to do as a woman. I knew that growth could sometimes hurt, and I figured that's what was happening to me every time I assessed my life and found myself feeling trapped. What I didn't consider was that I was making the same mistakes all over again, because surely, I would have learned my lesson by now. But no, yet again I was forcing myself to compromise because I wasn't sure yet what I wanted out of a relationship. Though it hurt, it had never occurred to me that pushing the issue with Badr was an option. We had disagreements about it, of course, but in truth I had other things on my mind besides his supposed infidelity.

I was convinced that Badr was always honest with me. A polygamous lifestyle, as half-hearted as it was on my part, required a lot of juggling to maintain. When we met, Badr was living with another woman whom he had two kids with. In fact, during a trip to Africa, the family of the mother of his children was the one who watched my kids. I even got her permission before I said "yes" and Badr and I went to the mosque. She agreed but was totally against it at heart; something I found out shortly thereafter when she tried to fight me. Prior to our marriage, I also knew that he was already legally married to another woman in order to obtain a green card so that he could stay in the USA. A marriage he told me was nothing to him but a union of convenience, and therefore nothing to worry about. When I met her, I knew that there was nothing between them except the big lie of the fake marriage. I felt sorry for the two of them being in such a gridlock, though I was also relieved by the fact that he was not trying to marry me to maintain his legal status. Instead, Badr assured me that our marriage was the result of pure love and nothing else.

In the beginning I was too excited about the possibilities and potential of our relationship to scratch beneath the surface. It hurts to admit, but I wasn't his first or his only. Instead, I was just another in a long line of women that he kept at his disposal. There was truth to the rumors. There had been all along. Badr tried to explain things away at first, and for a while I listened. I wanted to believe in him. I knew what it was to be cheated on and betrayed and I didn't want to think that I'd been silly enough to fall for it again. I'd done so much growing since leaving Seth that knowing that Badr was no better was a slap in the face. It was as if I'd betrayed myself, and it hurt as much as—if not more than—realizing that Badr wasn't who I'd hoped he'd be. Like our wedding ceremony, our relationship hinged entirely on what he valued and believed and left little room for what was important for me and my happiness. Looking back on our wedding, the day was more like a joke than something sacred or special. April fools! Damn if I didn't feel like to the fool of the decade!

It came as no surprise then that our union didn't even last a year. I still remember the day the woman he'd been living with came to my house. Part of his lifestyle included spending time with each of the women in his life, and as a result we all had assigned days that we spent with Badr. It was supposed to help us avoid westernized ideas like jealousy. Of course, it didn't work, which was how I found myself having a catfight with one of the people I was sharing my husband with. What the fight was about didn't matter. What made the moment so significant was that I couldn't recall how I'd found myself there. It was like waking up from a dream, except reality was the *Jerry Springer Show* and I was an unwilling guest on the stage that was my life.

I wasn't the type of person who got into fights over a man. Slapping and pulling hair to keep something that wasn't what I needed or wanted. I'd been raised better than that, had wanted more for myself than that, and yet there I was. It was like an out-of-body experience and I didn't recognize the person that I saw. By this time my youngest was four years old and I was forced to ask myself if Badr was really the kind of person that I wanted my son modeling himself after.

Even so, this was my marriage and I was determined to make it work. If it all fell apart, it wouldn't be because I didn't try. Too many people, including me, cling to mistakes because of the time and effort that they've expended in making them. First it was Reggie, then it was Seth, and finally Badr. I told myself that I was doing what was best for my children each time, never realizing that by hurting myself I was depriving them of the one stable, sturdy figure they had. There was only so much that I could do when I was pouring from an empty cup, though I was convinced that it only required a little extra effort on my part in order to get through the tough times.

It was second nature for me to assume that any hardship in my life could be overcome if *I* did more. It took a long time for me to realize that I couldn't solve everything and that sometimes trying to do so did more harm than good. That was the case with Badr. Polygamy was something I never would have approved of, and yet there I was, in a group relationship with several other people and somehow just as lonely as I'd been before Badr and I had started dating.

Love isn't supposed to make you lonely; it's supposed to fulfill you. The right relationship will make all the searching you did up until that point worthwhile. Maybe that was why I found it so hard to let Badr go. There was a part of me that didn't quite believe in true love and soul mates anymore, but desperately needed to. I'd grown up in an era where the idea of struggle love was everywhere. Love was supposed to hurt, you were supposed to sacrifice for it, and sometimes that meant forgiving a man if he started fooling around behind your back for the sake of your kids.

I told myself that I had it easy. He wasn't using me. I was with him because I chose to be. We were in love. I'd never felt this way about anyone before and surely the good times we'd shared meant that we were strong enough as a couple to work through the bad. So, what if he often acted nonchalant about the women he was sleeping with causally?

All I did know was that my life and emotions were in chaos. The more I tried to pretend as if everything was alright, the more it all fell apart. It was like standing on the edge of the coast. I could see the tide coming in and every time I thought I was far enough back; the ocean would sweep over my legs and drag more sand from beneath my feet. I was supposed to be standing still, but the world was being pulled out from under me and I was powerless to stop it. Everything about my relationship with Badr lacked harmony and balance. Time and time again, *I* was the one forced to give up pieces of myself. Though Badr made it all sound normal, the truth was that I *felt* as if I were being cheated on. His dalliances were blows that became harder and harder to simply brush aside.

Finding out about his other girlfriends was a blessing in a way, despite the hurt it caused me. Thank God that I was able to finally come to my senses and pull out of that mess. If I had left it up to him, we would have all been in that circus forever. After our separation—or divorce if you will—his lifestyle began to catch up with him. Badr was really on a downward spiral, doing one irrational thing after another, especially when it came to women. Mary, the lady he had two children with and who he was living with, told me that they eventually lost their house and that Badr married yet another woman in the mosque. Furthermore, despite Badr's attempts to stay in the country by putting a ring on it, with the "legal" wife, his plans ultimately fell through and he was eventually deported. Having him out of my life was a weight off my shoulders. I didn't have to force myself to conform to a way of life that went against the very core of who I was. Though once I realized that that's what I'd been doing, I had to ask myself why? Why was I always bending over backward to keep these men in my life? When I loved, I loved hard. I gave it my all. But did that have to come at the expense of who I was?

There's a fairy tale that you might be familiar with called "Cinderella." In it, Cinderella's ugly stepsisters are so eager to find love and be the one chosen by the Prince that when he comes to their home to determine if either can fit the glass slipper, they resort to drastic measures. One sister cuts off her toes, the other her heel. The ruse works at first, but then the shoe becomes so filled with blood that the sisters are found out one after the other and cast aside.

Love often made me feel like an ugly stepsister. I was always cutting away bits and pieces of myself, sacrificing the very things that kept me upright, throwing away the parts that didn't fit the mold I'd been told would be my only path towards happiness. I was afraid that one day, I would have cut away so much that there would be little of me left to recognize. I was already beginning to see it, starting with the fight I'd had with Badr's other conquest. The simple fact that I'd agreed to marry Badr devoid of both my God and family should have been hint enough that I was giving up too much. Instead, that sacrifice had simply bled into all the others, until one day I looked up and didn't even realize how I'd found myself in the position that I was in.

This couldn't happen again; I needed a common denominator. A variable that I could use to determine when and if I was going too far. It occurred to me that my passions often deceived me. Whenever I found myself in a toxic relationship, it was because I hadn't been thinking at all, too busy feeling like these men's prize possession to pay attention to what was happening. It would have been different had I been thinking with my heart *and* my head. If I were ever going to trust a man again, if I were ever going to risk my heart and the stability of my children again, then I needed to be smarter.

That's where Asad comes in.

Asad wasn't the result of passion. Our dynamic was the complete opposite, in fact. We started dating because—unlike Badr—Asad had the enthusiastic support of my family. I'd seen what happened when I dated men that they didn't approve of, and clearly, I wasn't as discerning as I'd like to believe. They pushed the idea of Asad onto me and after the roller coaster that was Badr, I needed the stability and care that he offered. I was tired of being swept off my feet only to land on my backside. Reggie groomed me into the perfect target, Seth had left me wounded, and Badr had poured salt into that wound. Asad was meant to give me time to heal fully from them all. I needed someone that I could lean on until I found my bearings once more, someone that I could trust. Asad was my safety net. Though there was no passion on my part, Asad and I got along very well. He listened to what I had to say, he never belittled me, and even my friends noticed that he treated me as if I were royalty.

Asad had all the benefits of dating Badr with none of the danger. He presented himself as honest and reliable: everything the men in my past hadn't been. Asad was more of a friend than a lover, and while I knew the spark would never be there, that didn't stop me from seeing him regardless. I grew to love him, but I was never *in love* with him and maybe that's what dulled the sting of finally learning the truth.

If I've learned anything over the years, it's that people can say one thing to your face and be living an entirely different life behind your back. That was Asad. It turned out that he too had a wife that I didn't know about. A wife he seemed all too happy to ignore while he was busy pursuing me. This was a different sort of hurt. It wasn't like the pain Badr and Seth had given me, but that didn't mean that the ache was any less. In all honesty, I was glad for it. Because it was Asad. I had turned down his proposal on more than one occasion, so I was still able to forgive once the shock of being lied to again had worn off. It helped that I had never seen him as a serious partner, and despite his lie we remained friends long after his skeletons came out of the closet.

It wasn't all bad. I gained my keys that day and they gave me the ability to reaffirm who I was. I am a loveable person deserving of a healthy, honest, and fulfilling relationship. I knew for a fact that Asad could not provide this and that I deserved better. It was time to stop cheating myself.

Reflections

I'm sure you're wondering what the point of all of this was.

That's certainly the thought that was going through my mind at the time. It's hard to know, even now, where life might have taken me had I stayed with either man. What I do know is that being with them taught me some invaluable lessons about myself and what I wanted in life. Being with them taught me what I was willing to put up with to reach that fabled happiness I'd been striving to find for so long and just how tenuous it could be when pursued blindly. I would like to say that the revelation was sudden, blinding, but in all honesty, it came to me in stages.

Any lesson worth learning reveals itself in parts. It's a lot like a person in that regard. You can never fully grasp the full extent of what something is trying to teach you when it comes all at once. It can be overwhelming, the truth of it too hard to swallow to ever genuinely appreciate. Up until that point in my life I had been absorbing life advice like a sponge. I knew what I should do, what would make my life easier, but knowing and doing it often turned out to be two separate things. I found myself looking back on a situation and wondering "why?"

Why had I done that?

Why had I said this?

Why didn't I confront him sooner?

Why did I put up with something when it so clearly made me unhappy?

Why? Why? Why?

That's when it came to me.

I could be the smartest, most intuitive person in the world, but none of it would matter until I started to see myself as such. It wasn't enough to simply put up boundaries; no, I had to demand more from myself and the people I allowed into my life. One way that I began to do that was through the power of affirmations. I refer to these affirmations as the keys.

~ Reaffirm yourself daily. ~

Chapter 6: *The Keys*
THE KEEPER OF THE DOORS

> *Gratitude unlocks the fullness of life. It turns what we have into enough, and more. It turns denial into acceptance, chaos to order, confusion to clarity. It can turn a meal into a feast, a house into a home, a stranger into a friend. Gratitude makes sense of our past, brings peace for today and creates a vision for tomorrow.*
> *—Melody Beattie*

One in five women and one in seventy-one men will be raped at least once in their lives. Meanwhile one out of every three women and one out of every six men will experience some form of sexual violence. 51.1% of women reported that an intimate partner was to blame, while 40.8% were attacked by an acquaintance. On the other side of the coin, 52.4% of men are raped by an acquaintance while 15.1% are assaulted by strangers.[4]

Rape is, for lack of a better word, a pandemic that continues to spread.

These numbers were never meant to frighten anyone or to trivialize. If you've ever experienced an assault—or any kind of

---

[4] Available at: https://www.nsvrc.org/statistics as of 5/2020.

violence—you are more than just a statistic. More than just a number. Knowing that I was one of many rape victims used to make me think differently. If rape was such a normal occurrence, then what made my situation so special? Why was it such a big deal? Why was it affecting me so much? Why couldn't I just...get over it?

This mindset is what brought me back to Reggie time and time again even after what he did to me. It's no surprise that he treated me like a piece of shit whenever we were together. Whenever he inserted his shrimp dick inside of me, I grew sick with nausea. It is almost as if each time I went back I was trying to convince myself that I wasn't being violated. I was trying to right the wrong. Otherwise, how could I live with myself? These feelings of shame and guilt—no, of blatant denial—are what encouraged me to reach out and insist that he have a relationship with China. Even though that fool didn't want anything to do with our daughter. At the time she was six years old, bright as candlelight and starting to ask questions about "dad."

Eventually, I got tired of hiding the truth.

Without thinking, I gathered her up and traveled to the address I'd found through child support during our latest hearing—a hearing which he did not show up for. I hastily climbed the stairs with her trailing behind cluelessly. I knocked on the door and when he opened it, I stormed in.

"China," I said. "This is your dad."

His eyes—already slightly bulging—almost popped out of his sockets. We spent some very awkward moments in silence and then an even more agonizing amount of time trying to start a dialogue. Eventually, he said that he would get to know her. What I didn't realize is that I had just invited King Hellraiser into our lives. Be careful what you ask for. Take heed of those old words of wisdom. No matter how hard you try, or how many fairy tales you read, you cannot turn a frog into a prince. This naivete is what blinded me to the many ways in which I was subconsciously attracting more betrayal into my life. Every time I succeeded at a goal, every time I excelled where someone told me I would fail, I saw it as proof that I was healing. Someone who was broken couldn't do what I did. Someone who was operating from a place of hurt couldn't have the life I'd built for myself from the ground up. But that's just the thing. Success doesn't equate to health any more than failure does to worth. If that were the case, then depression wouldn't be so prevalent in every walk of life.

I wasn't healed.

I was just on hold.

In the United States, more than one-third of women who reported being raped before eighteen subsequently experienced rape once again as an adult. Yet one more thing that I had Reggie to thank for, I suppose. In addition to the sexual assaults as a teenager and adult, I experienced other traumas as well that defined much of my life. Now that I'm older and wiser, I can look back on some of the things I went through and see what a large role my assault and other traumas played in my life. In many ways the repercussions of Reggie's violence are echoing even to this day.

Because of the pain I experienced as an adult, there were still times when I couldn't help but feel as if I would always be the victim. It's such a hard moniker to shake once you adopt it the first time. Once you've lived with it for so long you find yourself taking on those characteristics. It's a constant battle to shake those habits, to escape that "victim mindset." Many never even realize that it's a battle they're fighting because they haven't done the work to recognize the war going on within themselves.

Though Reggie is the father of my child, I realized that is where his influence in my life had to stop. China had that unconditional love for him as her daddy and I would never take that from her, even though I hated the way he always tried to turn her against me. The dynamic between the three of us taught me that when it comes to life, the relationships that you form are so nuanced and valuable to what it means to be a fully realized human being. I entertained relationships with people I would never want as part of the story of my life for the sake of those I loved. Though I don't regret it for an instant, those relationships took their toll on my emotional and physical well-being.

I was trapped in a miasma, a sea of past hurts, and I couldn't pull myself free of them.

There's a fine line between doing the work to overcome your trauma and learning to cope well enough to push it to the back of your mind. I had been so caught up in trying to be a good mother, provide for my family, go to school, and trying to juggle all of these different expectations I had for myself—and that society had for me—that I never took the time to let myself heal. I never took the time to put in the work to understand who *I* was and what *I* needed. It was years before I realized that "being healed" was necessary and should have been at the top of my self-development menu. After all, when you're born in trauma, living in trauma, and all you saw was trauma—well, it all becomes just a normal part of life. Something that's much easier to spot from the outside looking in. You may feel some urge that never seems to get settled. It may be your soul begging you to roll up your sleeves and get on the path to healing so that you can start to attract healthy, whole, and happy relationships without the scars and bruises from traumas, fears, and pains.

The connections you make in life often mirror what's going on inside, and that's why *the keys* are so important. The keys in our purses symbolize affirmations. I am not talking about those affirmations that merely validate our current existence. The definition of affirmations that I am speaking about are those that create our future. These kinds of affirmations naturally lead us right to gratitude. These are the kinds of affirmations that brought about the light bulb, automobiles, the latest fashion trends, and even the Internet. All these things were once considered impossible and there was a time, not long ago, when a person who imagined such inventions would have been institutionalized in an insane asylum for even thinking of such things out loud.

Without positive affirmations, many of the advancements we have now wouldn't even exist. It was the hope and vision for something better that brought about the change these innovators wished for. It works the same way when it comes to other aspects of life. Like they say, you attract what you put out and if you're coming from an unhealthy place, then more than likely the relationships you cultivate will also be unhealthy. Badr and Asad were a wake-up call. I didn't want my past to haunt my present or my future any longer. All the people that had hurt me, especially Reggie, were chapters that I needed to close, doors that I needed to shut if I ever had any hope of moving on.

When one door closes, another opens.

How often have you heard someone say those exact words?

I used to think that I knew what that phrase meant. From a practical standpoint, it's clear. The loss of one opportunity often heralds the arrival of a new and better one. It's a message that encourages you to remain hopeful, one that reminds us of the power of resilience. But there's a deeper meaning to it that I like to utilize in my private practice that has helped hundreds of people over the years.

The proverbial "doors" can represent many things, but now I consider them to be emotional pathways. Every door that you step through is a revelation on your path to ultimate self-enlightenment. But, like any door, you need the right key to open it and step across that threshold. The experiences that you have equip you with a set of keys. It's up to you to determine which keys open which doors, and which ones don't even belong on your key chain and which ones you need to add to it.

Asad and Badr gave me one of the most important tools in my arsenal.

The right key.

The one I needed to unlock the door to my affirmations about who I really am and what I really want in a relationship with myself and others.

I was so frustrated with everything that had happened that it forced me to take a close look at myself. Something I'd only ever done in small bursts. These brief moments of reflection were part of my healing at the time. They forced me to make decisions about what I was willing to put up with and whether I could do better. It's what drove me to dump Seth, to travel, to take up social work, and so forth. But it wasn't enough. Not anymore. I was ready to evolve as a woman. To grow. In order to do so I needed weapons, daily reminders that I could pull forth and brandish like a sword and shield whenever I found myself in a situation that threatened my ideals and goals.

I broke cycles and overcame great struggles even before I started to use affirmations at the conscious level, and that encouraged me like nothing else could. If I could do so much without them, how much more could I do with them in my back pocket? In order to determine what affirmations would be the most effective, I took a step back to assess the woman I'd grown to recognize as Montrella.

What were some of the things I found myself struggling with?

Well, I had a few trust issues for one. I was constantly struggling with my identity. Thanks in large part to the spiritual annihilation I'd experienced at the hands of first Seth and then Badr. I was vulnerable and prone to trying to prove my worth thanks to the emotional and mental abuse I'd undergone with Seth and Reggie. The numerous betrayals I'd experienced had changed me in more ways than I realized.

Each transgression was one more thing that chipped away at my confidence and sense of self. One more thing that I needed to examine in order to heal from. There were a lot of little moments like that. Where I had to comb through the various sacrifices and betrayals; some were committed by others against me, but most of them were crimes I'd committed against myself. A merry-go-round of indirect self-harm. In much the same way that a man might commit suicide by cop, I was self-sabotaging by lover.

Deep down the things that had been done to me had left me with the belief that I deserved what I was going through. After that final heartbreak, it took a conscious reminder that that wasn't true. What I deserved was something so much better than what I'd gotten so far. After a lot of trial and error, I was finally able to forgive Asad and Badr.

Dealing with Asad was proof that I could move past something without compromising more than I was willing to. It also showed me that I could have someone who hurt me in my life, so long as they didn't overstep any emotional boundaries that I may have set in place. Once I understood that the work needed to start with me and that I needed to remind myself every day of my own worth, it became easier to find the pieces of me that I'd lost and given away over the years. My keys gave me the wisdom to see what I genuinely wanted in a romantic relationship and to be honest with myself about if the relationship was a match with my desires. They also gave me the strength to then walk away from that relationship if the mold I found myself in wasn't where I wanted or needed to be.

I'm strong, resilient, and intelligent.

I accomplish anything that I put my mind to.

I deserve love and kindness and give it in return.

I am not *a victim.*

These reminders changed as I did, but there was never a moment when a deep breath and a couple of recitations of my personal mantra failed to bring me back on track whenever I strayed. Knowing myself realigned me with my purpose and my faith and, as a result, change came.

This time, for the better.

During the custody dispute over our son, Seth and his ignorant lawyers catered in lies in their attempt to get the judge to rule in their favor. Ironically, he tried to use my faith as his major premise as to why I should not have custody. Meanwhile, he was squatting in his friend's dirty studio. In addition to his illegal residence, he was also never held accountable for the abuse of two of his other children whose mothers were so influenced by Seth that they still allowed their children to be around him unsupervised despite said abuse. It was, and remains, a sad situation. His attorneys either knew the ugly truth and ignored it or were really that stupid even after years of law school. The custody battle for my son was ugly and expensive, but I can look back and say that I held my ground. I think their end goal was to leave me broke financially, mentally, and spiritually. Instead, their attack only made my faith stronger. Their mission accomplished—NOT! It was a shining example of me at my best; I had to know who I was and be willing to fight for that woman for the sake of my son—who has a real chance in this world. If I hadn't stood up for myself, the only thing the courts would have known about me was the foolish baloney that Seth fed them. And he claims to not eat meat? Bullshit! The man is full of swine!

In the end, my faith meant that victory over Seth's slander was inevitable. I celebrate that fact; you damn right I'm not a victim! I am a survivor with a full and beautiful life worth living.

I keep that knowledge close to my heart. It's what I use as proof when the occasional bouts of depression and anxiety try and tell me that I'm worthless and undeserving. I take that moment and study the bits of my character that shone through the brightest when the people I loved the most were threatened, and it helps me grow stronger. Since then, I've advanced mentally, spiritually, and emotionally by leaps and bounds.

And Seth?

Well, Seth is still jobless and out riding his bike with no shirt on to show off his six-pack, spouting off about the innate divinity of the black man while being blind to his own shortcomings. There's a lesson to be found there as well; namely that without doing the work, there's no such thing as moving forward. Instead, you will be stuck in your past.

RECIPE #3 - The "New Year New Me" Cobbler

Knowing yourself can be the sweetest reward after what might feel like years' worth of prep time. Remember that the time and effort you've put in so far wasn't in vain. This can be a difficult dish to master but putting in the work will guarantee a dessert you'll be proud to show off.

Prep Time: Lifelong   Serving Size: 1 to 2

Directions:

1. Create a new self-image that you fall madly in love with! It's time to look in the proverbial mirror. Who do you see there looking back at you? If it isn't someone, you're proud of, then it's time to make some serious changes. Take the time to write out your top four values. When you assess your life, how often are you compromising one or more of them? If health is important to you, then you can't eat McDonald's every day. This isn't just about reflection, but accountability.
2. Cut, cut, cut. Cut ties with toxic people, cut out old habits, and cut the excuses. You can't heal if you can't acknowledge the hurt and part of that is accepting your role in where you currently find yourself. Like dicing onions, this part can get a little messy but it's well worth a few shed tears.
3. Healing takes time. This isn't a marathon. You can't run a race without figuring out where the finish line is. What does recovery look like to you? What does one's healing look like? Where do you want to be mentally and spiritually tomorrow? Next week? Next year?
4. Give yourself a round of applause from time to time. Take it one step at a time. Acknowledge your achievements as you reach them, no matter how small. For some, progress is landing a new job or breaking away from a bad relationship. For others it's self-care and getting a full night's sleep. Once you understand what healing represents for you, it's easier to celebrate the milestones you reach on your way there.

5. Start with forgiveness on the home front. Healing is a deeply personal process and we often forget that it begins not on the outside, but on the inside. People like to tout the importance of forgiving other people, for instance, but rarely talk about what forgiving yourself looks like. A lot of people do just that, often forgiving others and never forgiving themselves when we're the ones who need that closure the most. Maybe it's because we forget that forgiveness begins with learning to love yourself once again. You're only human and your mistakes don't define who you are. Even if you make a life change only to turn around and slip up the very next day, don't sweat it. You can spend your whole life beating yourself up for every slip up or you can learn from it, grow from it, and move on. The whole point of healing is about moving on. Like stagnant water, sitting around and holding on to every "what if" or "if only" breads disease and attracts pests. You're better than that and you deserve better than that. It's just time that you realized it too.

Additional Notes: (Repeat daily or as often as needed. Can be used individually for some much-needed nourishment between meals.)
"I'm the only one responsible for my success and happiness.
~ I am self-aware and self-actualizing.
~ I forgive myself and today is the day I will strive to live my best life.
~ If I see something needs changing or doing, I take action quickly and responsibly."

Nutritional Facts - Per Serving
- 70% Self-Awareness
- 30% Acceptance

10/10 - Would Recommend

~ See yourself.
Know yourself.
Love yourself. ~

PART TWO: TO DO

> *What are you doing?*
> *A man who stands for nothing will fall for anything.*
> *—Malcolm X*

~ *Do Love!* ~

Chapter 7: *The Panty Liners*

Sweeping it Under the Rug

> *The mistake ninety-nine percent of humanity made,
> as far as Fats could see, was being ashamed of what
> they were; lying about it, trying to be somebody else.*
> —J.K. Rowling, The Casual Vacancy

You're 16, and he's the love of your life.

He says that he'll never leave you. That you're his forever.

Mostly, he tells you that no one will ever love you the way that he does. When you find out you're pregnant and he leaves, you still believe him though you aren't sure why.

You're 23, and your boyfriend doesn't enjoy beating you, but you always seem to make him mad. You have kids together and finding a better job while juggling what it means to be a mother seems impossible when you have to keep him happy on top of everything else. You know you should dump him, but it is hard. You're used to the abuse, but you're not used to being alone and lonely, and the latter is more frightening than anything that you can imagine.

You're 30, and your husband is cheating. You promised yourself that you would never be that person, that woman, that puts up with that sort of disrespect, but what else are you supposed to do? You've invested time and money into this relationship, stuck with him when he was struggling, and been the voice of reason when he broke down. All for what? A litany of broken promises and half-realized dreams. You're not going to throw away years of effort and loyalty because of one mistake.

Or two.

Or three.

I could go on and on, but I'm pretty sure you get the point. It might be familiar to you, that moment when you look up and realize that you aren't happy and probably haven't been for a good, long while. That moment when you must decide to stay or to go, already knowing the answer but unwilling to accept it for fear of what it might mean. Maybe you have been there before, or maybe you know someone who has. Either is just as likely because unless you're particularly lucky in love, most of us have had our fair share of bad relationships.

I've heard it all before and the tale might hit closer to home than you think.

Girl meets boy, boy hurts girl, and girl—inexplicably—stays. By now every story, every relationship, is as familiar to me as my own. So familiar, in fact, that I decided to write a book about it. The romantic mishaps that defined my younger years taught me some tough lessons, but they also gifted me with a level of empathy that has benefitted hundreds of my clients over the years.

When you are in the middle of a difficult situation, it's impossible to imagine that someone else understands what you're going through. Advice seems to hit differently when the person giving it has similar experiences to pull from. There were so many well-meaning—and not so well-meaning—people who tried to tell me to walk away from Seth. If anything, their advice sounded more like judgment, and I went out of my way to make excuses for why I had to stay or why things were not as bad as they seemed to think. If I had listened sooner, there is no doubt that my life would have turned out differently though I can't say that I regret the paths that I took to get to where I am. Still, there are a lot of things that I know now that I wish I had known back then. While I cannot go back and change the past, I can do better moving forward because I've learned to recognize my patterns and own up to the self-destructive behavior that kept dragging me back to square one.

When it comes to relationships, many of us have been there at one point or another where we have found ourselves wondering why we were trying to stay with someone who was no good for us. We have found ourselves wondering how we got to a point where our happiness was something that had to be bartered for the sake of someone else's parody of love. Most of all, we have all found ourselves doing something that we regret.

But why?

Why stay? Why put up with all the hurt and disrespect in the first place? Lack of resources? Low self-esteem? Perhaps there are children involved? For too many the thought of disrupting the household may seem worse than anything they have learned to put up with. In several cases, it's a combination of all three. This is especially true when physical or emotional abuse plays a large role in the family dynamics.

Abuse of any kind is the leading issue affecting most relationships today. Domestic violence, for instance, is an epidemic and touches the lives of one in four women and one in seven men. On average that is about twenty people per minute, which amounts to more than ten million men and women a year. If that isn't bad enough, it takes the average victim over two years to seek help.

Two years.

Two years of hiding an ugly truth. Two years of cleaning up the mess to present a pretty face to the world. Two years of hiding. Two years of sweeping it all under the rug and mopping up the mess rather than facing an all too harsh truth. A truth that demands facing the heart of the problem instead of only cleaning it up and hoping that next time, things won't be so bad.

For many, that two years can feel like an eternity. Even a few months can mean the difference between life or death. In some cases, even the women who survive are not completely unscathed. While emotional abuse can be harder to quantify because of its subtleties, the numbers are no less staggering. It can wear on your physical health and demolish your self-esteem. It can also tear families apart and leave lasting impressions on any children unlucky enough to be caught in the middle. Both emotional and physical abuse are so ingrained in our culture that seeing depictions of toxic relationships in the media as if they were the standard has become normal. It's easy to dismiss the everyday cruelty you experience because the world has told you that it's just the way that things are—that violence equals passion, and couples often say cruel things to one another in the spirit of witty dialogue.

In case no one has ever told you, none of that is normal.

Or at least it shouldn't be. It certainly doesn't *have* to be.

Panty liners are things that, women have learned to keep hidden away. We carry them with us everywhere we go, tucked deep in the recess of our purse. They are always there at the back of our minds, ready just in case there's yet another mistake to keep secret. They help us clean up those intimate messes that all too often crop up. Those messes that prompt shame or embarrassment when they've been left exposed to public scrutiny for too long.

Don't get me wrong.

When it comes to the art of discretion, those panty liners can be a wonderful teacher, but they shouldn't be the tool that you reach for when you're having relationship issues. A lot of my clients have a hard time seeing the light at the end of the tunnel. Even more of them have a hard time realizing that there is a tunnel to get through in the first place. For too many of us, the bad has become such a natural way of life that we can't recognize it for the poison it is, so we just keep choking it down and calling it water. It sometimes takes stepping away from a situation to fully grasp just how damaging it's been. Yet, stepping back from a problem long enough to gain the perspective you need is sometimes harder than leaving could ever be.

Growth can be painful, thus "growing pains," so don't be surprised if gaining a new perspective on your love life can trigger feelings of shame and regret. For some, these feelings make it impossible to see where they can make quality changes for the better. Addicts and women who have had abortions, for instance, are especially susceptible to this line of thinking. The belief that what they've done is unforgivable, or that it somehow makes them unworthy of love or respect can be impossible to ignore. This is when the art of self-awareness becomes confused with self-deprecation and ends up doing more harm than good. It's important to realize that lying to yourself isn't always denying that there's anything wrong to begin with. It's also telling yourself that there's no doing any better once you've accepted that there's a problem. When you lie to yourself and keep everything tucked away rather than confronting it head-on, you hinder your own healing.

Remember, the trick to healing and doing better for yourself and the people you love is learning to forgive yourself. So many women are ashamed of the path that life has led them down that they find it difficult to take personal responsibility for their addictions, both literally and figuratively. And being mistreated *can* be addictive. Like a drug, those brief moments of happiness help outweigh the inevitable, crushing lows that come once the high has gotten the chance to wear off.

Forgiving yourself is one of the most important things that you can do because it requires first being honest with yourself. Throughout the course of this book you've picked up several recipes designed to help you learn how to self-reflect with kindness and authenticity. Take those tools and reassess whatever situation you've found yourself in. Is it a break from your norm or just another mistake in what has become a pattern?

Confront what you can't deal with. Whether it's infidelity, abuse, a decision that you regret, or a personal flaw that you just can't shake. None of these situations has the power to undermine your worth unless you allow them to. Remember your affirmations and your recipes so that at the end of the day you have the wherewithal to demand better for yourself when it comes to picking a partner and breaking hurtful habits. Once you've learned to see things for what they are rather than what your self-esteem has painted them, there's no end to the number of changes that you can make.

ACTION STEP FOR SUCCESS: Confrontation

Method: See things for what they are so that you can acknowledge any decisions that you're making that contribute to your choice in men. Forgive yourself for the time and effort you've spent on this person and engage in behavior that coincides with your desires and goals.

Exercise: Write out what your life is like. What are you being told? How does the reality differ from what you want out of a romantic partner? If your goal is a relationship that cultivates loyalty and longevity, then entertain people who have the same aspirations. When your significant other shares your goals, then you never have to hide or sacrifice bits and pieces of yourself to fit into the mold they've created for you. Set yourself up for success by aligning your reality with your wants and needs rather than the other way around. Remember that it takes courage to confront what's holding you back and learning from it. If you never take the time to confront your own trends, you'll keep finding yourself engaged in the same cycles.

~ Confront your relationship trends and learn from them. ~

Chapter 8: *Pepper Spray and Tissue*

STANDING YOUR GROUND

> *Guilt can prevent us from setting the boundaries that would be in our best interests, and in other people's best interests.*
> *—Melody Beattie*

We've touched base here and there about getting back what you put into relationships, but the same is the case for life in general. There's nothing as important to your mental and emotional well-being than a solid set of boundaries. Most of my problems both romantically and otherwise can be traced back to a lack of well-established boundaries. A part of it was naivete. I didn't understand myself and therefore it was hard to pinpoint when someone was crossing a line that would ultimately make me uncomfortable.

Reggie is the first example of how a lack of proper boundaries negatively impacted my life, though it was a recurring theme in one way or another in every relationship that followed. What made boundaries so difficult to establish was first understanding what they were and why they were important.

One day while I was wandering through the store, I came across a miniature tube of pepper spray. I kept it in my purse for years and while I never needed to use it, having it close by gave me a sense of security. In the back of my mind I knew that if someone ever made me uncomfortable or afraid, I could pull it out and defend myself and my personal space. That small measure of protection gave me confidence to go places I may have otherwise been too frightened to venture.

Your boundaries are your emotional pepper spray. They give you confidence to step outside of your comfort zone, to explore not only what you don't need but to lay claim to what you do. I used to be so in love with Seth—and then Badr and Asad—that I allowed them to walk all over my boundaries. Ultimately sacrificing bits of myself until there was no recognizing the woman I had become. It took years to find myself again, a process I never would have had to engage in had I stayed true to who I wanted to be.

For those of you who have found yourself in a similar position, take a moment and ask yourself if what you're feeling is actually love? Love is meant to enhance your life, not diminish your sense of self. Always bending over backward for the sake of another person can play havoc with your confidence, which can lead to making other poor choices in love down the road.

Let's paint a picture:

You hook up with a man you met, and the two of you hit it off. There's an obvious connection but he tells you that he isn't looking for anything serious while simultaneously treating you like his significant other. He grows jealous when you show interest in other men and is annoyed when you seem equally jealous of his dalliances. As time passes the constant back-and-forth starts to affect your emotions. You find yourself comparing other men to him, and even though you're single, it doesn't feel that way. If this scenario sounds at all familiar, then you're beginning to understand exactly why boundaries can be so important when it comes to life and love.

Boundaries aren't just about protecting your limits from other people, but also setting limits for yourself. You have to understand going in exactly how much you're willing to put up with. That starts by determining what it is that you're hoping to get out of the relationship in the first place. If you're hoping for a husband, a white picket fence, and 2.5 kids, then booty calls and one-night stands have to become a thing of the past. Boundaries are powerful because they are associated with the need to have pride and respect in yourself. Without that sense of pride and self-respect it's easy to fall into the trap of allowing people to dictate your worth by their actions or lack thereof. Once someone has crossed a certain line, it's hard to bring them back to square one. It's a lot like making a first impression. Once that initial meeting has taken place, it's impossible to get that moment back. The pace of every encounter afterward will be determined by that of the first. That's why it's up to you to teach the world who you are and how you should be treated.

I always tell my clients not to allow an "ex" to take up any mental, emotional, or physical space. Namely because an ex is usually someone who has overstepped your boundaries. They've proven that they have no respect for how you need to be treated in a relationship and the more you allow them space in your mind, the more you undermine the limits that you set in place.

The best way to teach the world how you should be loved is to lead by example. How you treat yourself is often a guideline that others use to determine what you're willing to put up with and how far they can go. In a relationship this translates to a partner who is constantly taking advantage of their significant other. Every relationship should have an equal amount of give-and-take and if your partner is constantly taking from you, then it establishes an imbalance in your dynamic as a couple.

Like before, let's imagine a couple. Maybe the woman has a job, but the man doesn't. He promises that he's looking or that he has something in the works, but until he gets back on his feet, he just needs a little help. Before you know it "a little help" goes from a few dollars here and there for gas or groceries to you paying for his phone bill and car note while he sits on your couch eating your food and watching your cable.

Can I get an, "Amen"?

A wise woman once said, "No. I don't want no scrub. A scrub is a guy that can't get no love from me." And that's the kind of energy that you should be cultivating with every relationship whether it's newly established or one you've been working on for years. Never be afraid to demand better from the people around you, especially when it comes to romance.

You may be wondering how you can demand better if you aren't even sure what you want. For many, it's hard to imagine what a healthy relationship looks like if they've never had one. In these instances, it would be easy to mistake what should be the standard for someone going above and beyond. For example, being so used to McDonald's being treated as a date that going to Red Lobster or Applebee's feels like a luxury.

It's hard to tell yourself not to settle when you aren't sure where the bar should be set. That's where your self-assessment skills come into play. Don't establish your boundaries by someone else's standards and definitely not by society's standards—if such a thing even exists today; instead dig deep and ask yourself what you want out of a partner. What do you consider a deal breaker? What pushes you to succeed or simply pushes your buttons? At the end of the day, how do you want to feel when you're with your significant other?

Once you've established your boundaries and expectations, it's time to make some tough decisions. By now, you should be well equipped to not only identify your problems but to acknowledge the root cause of them. Now it's time to take things a step further and get out the *tissues*.

Figuratively, of course.

Like the panty liners, your tissues are there to help you clean up the mess. Unlike the former, however, tissues are meant to heal, not hide. The same way they wipe away tears, smeared makeup, and the occasional runny nose, the small packet of tissues you carry with you stops you from allowing your setbacks from becoming everyone else's problem.

It might seem strange to tie tissues and pepper spray together, but they go hand in hand. Without tissues, you run the risk of infecting others with the toxic habits you just cleansed from your system through the self-assessment needed to create your boundaries. Your tissues keep you from setting unrealistic goals that stemmed from past hurts and disappointments. To offer a bit of perspective, it's claiming that you want a good man only to turn around and punish that good man for the mistakes of all the bad ones who came before him. Your tissues allow you to establish what you want and need without going so far that you begin to self-sabotage your own love life.

Cleaning yourself up and throwing away what's no longer needed is an art, and it can take months, even years, of practice. It's also what makes the act of boundary building such a mercurial process. The boundaries that you set today may be completely different than what you put into place several years from now. The scope and rigidity of those boundaries directly reflects your state of mind from one relationship to the next. That's why it's so important to let go of certain people, ways, and codependent behavior. (More on that later.)

That's why you must keep tissues in your purse, ladies, because most likely the tears will flow as you let go of things, habits, and people that you have grown accustomed to your whole life. But this is a very necessary step. Because, when you fail to do so, the limitations that you set into place may do more harm than good. In fact, it may end up being impossible to stick to the changes you want to make in your life because you continually find yourself falling back into the same old habits with the same old people.

This part of the purse is all about breaking down old cycles. Once you have made up your mind that it's something you need and want to do, you'll find that it's easier than you think. I know from personal experience that it can be a hard pill to swallow. It took a long time before I was able to mentally and emotionally let Seth go. I was always envisioning how things could be. Once I started doing so, I noticed similarities between our relationship and other couples' panty liners. It showed me that Seth and I were not lining up with each other or with what I had envisioned for myself. I was forced to accept the fact that being with this man wasn't serving me, my children, or even Seth himself. Even then, it was hard to decide what I needed to do next because I was being lied to and manipulated. Still stubbornly clinging to that used napkin, I hadn't yet thrown away what was making me sick. I was still trying to convince myself that there was a way to make my reality coincide with my vision for the future.

But the pieces simply weren't fitting, and as soon as I accepted that, everything began to make sense. Decisions don't always happen in an instant; sometimes they're an evolution. Seth and I were existing in a state of codependency and I had to first break myself free of it before I could make any lasting changes. You can consider yourself codependent when another person's actions and behavior have an effect over you, and you continuously try and control them. It stems from addictions of any sort. It is a dysfunctional cycle that runs in families and romantic relationships more often than we want to admit. Codependency is characterized as a relationship where one person is responsible for meeting all their partner's excessive emotional and psychological needs. It's also a relationship that allows a person to continue addictive or irresponsible behavior by depending solely on their partner for financial, mental, and emotional support. It can be just as dangerous and all-consuming as any drug because it often demands just as much personal sacrifice. What makes it more devastating than anything you could buy on the street is the fact that you can convince yourself that the other person loves you and isn't simply using you.

Through trial and error, I've realized that it's your environment just as much as it is your circumstances and the people around you that play a role in creating and maintaining codependent relationships. It's up to you to determine which is the culprit and to break free. If you're in an environment that isn't conducive for your health and well-being as an individual first, then do whatever you need to in order to leave. If you're around people who make you feel as if you can't survive without them, leave. If your circumstances have limited you in any way, change them.

It's simple enough to say, but just like decisions, change is oftentimes a marathon instead of a sprint. Leaving and letting go can sometimes take years. Understand that codependency stems from some sort of addiction—either to a specific person or to how a certain situation makes you feel. Because of this, it creates dysfunction in relationships. The only way to end codependency is to first recognize the attributes of it.

Symptoms of Codependency

- Inability to follow through

- Harshly judging yourself and others

- Low self-esteem

- Projecting

- Inability to recognize, develop, and/or sustain "normal" and/or meaningful relationships

- Making others responsible for your emotions

- Inability to handle change

- Impulsivity

- Isolation

- Feelings of intense fear, inadequacy, anger, and so forth

- No sense of urgency when it comes to decision-making

- Constant need for approval/reassurances

- Can't tell the difference between love and pity

- Hero complex

- Almost pathological need to lie

- Willingness to endure abuse for the sake of love

- Tendency to "lose" yourself in love

Of course, this list is by no means complete. While it highlights some of the major symptoms associated with codependency, there's no ignoring the other red flags you may notice. Anytime your sense of self, or worth, is tied to how someone else perceives you, then there's a problem. Anytime you find yourself covering for someone's bad behavior at the risk of your own well-being and sacrificing everything you hold dear just to gain their approval, then it's time to take a step back. Anytime you feel guilty or unworthy when shown love or kindness, then it's time to reinvent yourself and your mindset.

Codependent relationships are everywhere, especially the media. For a while, that kind of blind devotion and reckless sacrifice was shoved down our throats as being what true love looked like. I can't tell you how many times I've watched something on Lifetime or even the Hallmark Channel and had to shake my head at what was being depicted. When you know what to look for, codependency is easy enough to spot. Once you do, the question then becomes how to let these habits go so that you can grow into who you were meant to be all along.

ACTION STEPS FOR SUCCESS: Decision-making and an ability to let go.

Method: Look at, and let go of, your old identity in order to re-invent the new. Our successes and failures play a huge role in how we face the world. The things that we excel at build confidence, while the areas where we struggle leave us questioning our capabilities. Together, these experiences shape our self-image, and consequently how we present ourselves to others. Therefore, self-reflection isn't just about questioning what you want and why. It's also about looking at the factors that shaped you and determining if they deserve to be the building blocks of your identity. How does the media depict the people that look like you? What do you remember of your childhood? What sort of people were your parents? Each of these factors plays a role in determining who we are.

Exercise: Who are you? More importantly, who do you want to be? The answer to both is harder to find for some than it is for others. It's what makes those online quizzes so popular. People are searching for answers, or at least a finger in the right direction. Knowing what kind of fruit, you'd marry, or which celebrity has a crush on you is an irreverent and lighthearted way of shedding light on an otherwise complex question, but in the end it you're still at square one. There's one self-image exercise that I share with my clients that has yielded promising results. If nothing else, it's definitely more helpful than a Buzzfeed article about your Harry Potter inspired soul mate. First, record 25 negative self-image statements that you lay claim to: "I'm ugly"; "I'm stupid"; "No one will ever love me." Once you're finished, rip it up and accept that these things aren't true. Now record 25 self-image statements that you want for yourself, like: "I'm attractive and loved." Then **let go** and **let God**.

Chapter 9: *Lip Gloss*

TELLING IT LIKE IT IS

> *Let us make a special effort to stop communicating with each other, so we can have some conversation.*
> —Mark Twain

If there is one thing that no woman has left out of her purse, it's a tube of lip gloss or Chapstick. That one item has been a staple for well-moisturized lips and relationships for decades. Our lips do so much for us. They kiss boo-boos and make them better, entice lovers, and express our happiness, sadness, or rage. Your lips are often one of the first things that someone notices about you, which is why they represent verbal and nonverbal communication.

Communication.

It's more than talking about your day at work or discussing your favorite television show. As an essential part of any relationship, communication calls for the exchanging of ideas. It's a process of giving and receiving that many women find themselves missing out on. Mainly because of the belief that communication is a one-way street. In my line of work clients often complain about their partners not listening to them when they speak, but they very rarely look at where they could be doing better. What I've discovered is that when there's a breakdown in communication, it's never just one person's fault. In the grand scheme of things there's always someone who isn't expressing themselves effectively, someone who isn't actively listening, or both.

I want to start off by saying that to communicate is not only about expressing yourself. It's also about listening to your partner and comprehending what you're being told so that you can understand where they're coming from. When someone speaks, are you absorbing what they're saying or are you just waiting for them to stop talking so that you can make your next point? Are you hearing everything they're trying to express or are you caught up in emotion over one little thing, thereby deafening yourself to the rest of the conversation? How do you communicate? How do you get your point across? Are you yelling? Using passive-aggressive language? Or do you engage with your partner through text and emoji, hoping that the lack of context and tone doesn't render your words obsolete?

First things first:

Yelling is not communicating.

Being passive-aggressive is not communicating.

Texting, despite its widespread use, is not communicating— though it can be easily mistaken as such, especially since a more tech-savvy generation has fallen out of the habit of speaking face-to-face. The problem there is that texting isn't personable and can often convey the wrong message if read differently than intended. In addition to removing a certain amount of personal accountability for anything that they may say through text, people also fail to consider that communication can mean something different to everyone. What communication means to you determines how you go about it with the people in your life. If your method doesn't coincide with someone else's, then they aren't likely to "get" you on any significant level. All combined, relying on your phone to convey your thoughts and emotions is asking for a perfect storm of misunderstandings and hurt feelings.

As a woman, it may be tempting to get out everything that's been weighing on you in a long, drawn-out text that took you several frenzied minutes to tap out. You stood in a parking lot or in the center of the grocery store glaring down at your phone and ignoring everything else around you while you desperately searched for the right words and phrases to convey the turmoil in your head. All for what? To get a one-word response or to find yourself left on "read"? It's a recipe for disaster and no matter how justified it may feel in the moment, none of my clients has ever reached any sort of emotional resolution from giving in to the temptation.

In the same way that our self-image is formed through our successes and failures, relationships are crafted through communication or lack thereof. If two people communicate in a more physical way, then that limits the scope of problems that they can address when sex is no longer an option.

When a woman finds herself in a one-sided, codependent relationship she is used up and neglected because she's failed to effectively communicate her boundaries in a healthy way. There are a few key phrases there to keep in mind. There's a difference between effective and healthy methods of communication and talking. When a woman can convey her thoughts and emotions in a way that her partner can accept and empathize with, that's healthy and effective communication. Raised voices and thrown insults isn't how two people in love should speak to one another, especially if that's the only way that they know how to air out their issues. Couples who can't tell the difference between talking to one another and talking *at* one another.

When someone in a volatile relationship has low self-esteem and finds themselves thrown aside, it can lower their esteem even further and create a domino effect on what sort of relationships they attract. One of the great things about your favorite tube of lip gloss? It's a way to regain control over yourself and an otherwise small moment in time. Reapplying lip gloss allows a woman to step fully into herself and who she is if only for a few seconds. From the scent, to the way the shade complements her skin tone, to the shape of her mouth. It's a stolen instance of quiet indulgence and mindfulness that boosts confidence in just a few seconds. You choose what lip gloss to wear that day based on how you feel and how you want others to experience you. It's a perfect example of the complexities of what it means to truly communicate. After all, a person who isn't confident or sure of what they want will never demand better from those around them.

They'll also never have the courage to speak up about what makes them unhappy because of the belief that they aren't good enough and perhaps even deserve what they get. Unlike some of the other items in our purse, lip gloss encourages a reaction from our partners as well. Everything from flavor to shade hints to him how you're feeling and where you're going. A more neutral shade, for example, tells those around you that you're feeling laid back and confident in your own skin while bright red lips are passionate and fierce. Communication is a two-way street that requires talking to one another, listening to your partner, and offering feedback to what was being said.

It's important to realize that couples don't always have the same style or speed of communication. Speed of communication is important because while the person you love may have already had an emotional revelation, it may take you a moment to get on the same page. Sometimes it might seem as if this delay is intentional and a sign of dismissal and apathy. This can lead to miscommunication and hurt feelings. When such an essential part of a relationship breaks down, it sets those involved up for regret.

Conversely, a woman can also be too confident. So much so that she crosses the line between who is the alpha in the relationship and who is the beta. Research suggests that a healthy relationship can't have either two alphas or two betas. It's the same concept that says that when dancing, one person must lead and the other must accompany them. It's a power dynamic seen often in nature, art, and music. When two equally strong presences are vying for control, chaos ensues. When a woman takes on an alpha role, she finds herself in the position of taking care of her partner and enabling the same negative behavior that she has a problem with. A woman who is used to playing the alpha in relationships will eventually meet up with a man who is also willing to claim that position, guaranteeing that the two will butt heads.

Just as damaging as conflicting love speeds, and an uneven flow of give-and-take, is when a couple has different love languages. A love language is the method by which a person expresses and feels love. There are five different types, and often one person's idea of love is different from that of their partners.

TYPES OF LOVE LANGUAGES

- <u>**WORDS OF AFFIRMATION**</u>—Those who respond to this love language require declarations of love and loyalty. They need to hear their partner say, "I love you," "I appreciate you," "Great job," and so forth. People in this category enjoy when their man talks about why he loves them and how much. A way to accomplish this is by being open and honest. This category isn't about offering up false platitudes or digging for compliments. If this isn't something your partner is doing, try leading by example and doing it first. If it makes them happy, that may be enough to encourage them to be more candid about their feelings as well.

- **PHYSICAL TOUCH**—Both calming and reassuring, this love language is the quickest way to express love and affection. People who express love through physical touch like holding hands, hugging, and so forth. Don't fall into the trap of thinking that all physical touch must be sexual in nature either. The Japanese promote the idea of skin ship—which involves touching and being touched by another person. For some, sex doesn't always equate to intimacy or a feeling of love. This is especially true for some victims of sexual abuse. If you're comfortable and your partner is willing, consider suggesting a few moments of skin ship a day. It allows you to become more present and aware of your own body, provides emotional comfort, and aids the libido in case things have begun to slow down in the bedroom. It can also just be nice to know that someone is there without the expectation of something more; soothing feelings of loneliness and the depression that often comes hand in hand with it.

- **QUALITY TIME**—Quality time is showing love via your undivided attention and can be the hardest to accomplish. With cell phones, work, chores, and other obligations to attend to it can be difficult to dedicate a few moments to the person you care about; but then again, that's what makes it so special in the first place. This is the love language that thrives on communication because it's when couples often take the time to sit down and open up to one another. Quality time can be something as simple as sitting on the couch and watching television to more intimate acts like making love or creating something together.

- **ACTS OF SERVICE**—This love language is all about the little things. Cleaning the house, putting gas in her car, massaging her shoulders. These small acts of kindness translate to love for

those who fall into this category, but those who do can sometimes feel as if they're asking too much. Those who gravitate
towards acts of service as a love language are usually individuals who haven't experienced many of these acts during the
course of their life. If no one has ever rubbed your feet after a
long day of work, then the first man who does it might be Mr.
Perfect as far as you're concerned. Whether you're used to being treated a certain way or not, never shy away from expecting
a lover to cater to you as if you hung the moon and the stars in
the sky. You deserve nothing less.

• <u>RECEIVING GIFTS</u> — If you've ever had a hard time shopping for
presents and someone said, "It's the thought that counts," just
know that they were right. At least when it comes to the men
and women who respond to this love language. People in this
category respond to the thoughtfulness and time that goes into
choosing a gift specifically for them. It's not about the money
but about the emotion that inspired the urge and the more spon-
taneous the act the better.

Some people can have more than one love language so it's important to speak to your partner to understand what works and
what doesn't. The act of discovering another person's love language often inspires a new attentiveness to them and their needs
that boosts communication. Anytime there have been problems in
my relationships, our communication was the first thing that un-
raveled. I realized just how important it was to talk, listen, and respond when I noticed how quickly things could fall apart otherwise.

When the individuals in a relationship are healthy and well
rounded, love languages can be a great place to start to reconnect.
It's when a person doesn't know who they are or what they want

that things begin to take a turn. A lack of proper boundaries can also taint a person's idea of love. It's all too easy for acts of service to be a form of enabling, while physical touch and quality time can be warped into clingy or obsessive behavior. Like everything we've discussed in this book, love languages require balance to benefit you and your loved one properly. A surefire way to accomplish that is through communicating, not only with your significant other but with yourself so that you can better understand what it is you're looking for out of a relationship and how you can respond to the needs of the person that you're with.

There are as many different forms of communication as there are couples out there. Unfortunately, there's no manual or step-by-step guide that teaches you how to speak to your significant other. But then, there doesn't have to be. When you're confident in yourself and know what you need to be happy, it's easier to convey those needs to the person you love. If all else fails, being attentive and showing them how you'd like to be cared for can go a long way towards opening the doors of communication. It's as much about how you approach a subject as it is what you say, so as long as you treat your partner with the same level of respect and care that you would expect in return, then there's no reason why you shouldn't be able to get your point across loud and clear. Effective communication skills are a useful tool to have and like your favorite brand of lip gloss it's something you should be able to take with you wherever you go.

ACTION STEPS FOR SUCCESS: Assess relationship and partner to determine one another's speed of communication and love language.

Method: It may seem obvious, but a person's personality plays a big role in what kind of communicator he or she is. If you're more introverted, you may express yourself in a completely different way than someone who's extroverted. Along with rate of speed and having a different love language from your partner, clashing personality types can also derail attempts at effective communication. While your intentions may be good, you can't fix something if you don't know what the problem is. So, start off with an assessment of your relationship to figure out what sort of communicators you and your partner are before actually trying to address any hard-hitting issues.

Exercise: Practice what communication means to you, both individually and within a partnership. Don't be afraid to take a communication class in order to understand the subtleties of it. Communicating effectively can be more complicated than you think, so don't underestimate the importance of mastering active listening when pride and hurt are trying to get in the way. Invest your time, money, and resources and be open and willing to go beyond your comfort zone. This isn't just about you, though cultivating your skills in this area will certainly help improve your relationship for the better. Being able to listen isn't just about hearing another person but doing so through whatever internalized filter you may have. These filters protect our pride and our feelings but can cause arguments and arguing is not a form of communication.

~ Effective communication is key. Cultivate your skills and each other's love language. ~

PART THREE: TO HAVE

What Can You Have?
I'm selfish, impatient and a little insecure. I make mistakes, I am out of control and–- at times–hard to handle. But if you can't handle me at my worst, then you sure as hell don't deserve me at my best.
—Marilyn Monroe

~ *Have Love!* ~

Chapter 10: *The ID*

FIND YOURSELF

Belladonna (n.) In Italian a beautiful lady; in English, a deadly poison. A striking example of the essential identity of the two tongues.
—Ambrose Bierce

I can recount every time I've ever lost my license.

Why?

It's just a piece of plastic with my information and picture on it. Yet, what makes it so simple is also what makes it so important. Losing my license has always been a big deal, not only because the experience itself was so stressful, but because of how hard I had to work to replace what I'd lost. You see, it was never the kind of incident that I could simply sweep under the rug and forget about. In fact, losing my ID was like losing a loved one in many ways. Each time I did it, I found myself going through the *Five Stages of Grief*:

1. **Denial**— *"It must be around here somewhere."*
2. **Anger**— *"Where the hell could I have put it?"*
3. **Bargaining**— *"If I could just find it, I swear I'll never drink again."*

4. **Depression**— *"What's wrong with me? Why wasn't I more careful?"*
5. **Acceptance**— *"Well, I guess I'll spend the next few hours stuck at the DMV."*

After a certain point, replacing my ID was no longer simply a question of devoting time and energy to its return. Eventually, I had to start paying for my own carelessness. In many ways, your license/ID has a lot in common with the mirror. The difference is that the mirror reflects what's there from one moment to the next. Your ID represents who you are at your core. Like a rookie baseball card, it lists your stats in unapologetic terms. You're this tall, you weigh this much, and this is what you look like when you forget to wear makeup on a Tuesday morning. It's the raw, basic ingredients of you that you go back to again and again. You use it to prove your identity to everyone you come across: your employer, the officer who pulled you over, the occasional waitress taking your order on margarita night.

Losing it is tantamount to losing yourself. In the wrong hands someone can strip that identity from you or use the information they find to invade your life in unhealthy ways. Metaphorically speaking, our ID fulfills the same purpose in our relationships. It serves as a method of accountability. How have we presented ourselves to our loved one, who have we claimed to be? Are we still living up to those same standards that we've set or are we faking it now just to get through the door?

Your ID is very much giving what you want to receive in return. What are you giving yourself up for? Who are you giving yourself to? Do they have a right to you or are they the emotional equivalent of an identity thief? In a healthy, authentic relationship two people can present their ID's to one another and know that what they're seeing is what they're going to get. It requires you to check in in a relationship and to be present and accountable. It's alright to give something worthwhile to receive a love that's worthy of you, so long as you always know how to reclaim yourself.

Your license gives you permission to step into places that you may not have been ready for before. That means that it isn't just about knowing yourself, it's also about knowing where you belong and where you're going in regard to love. Sometimes different ID's open different doors and allow you to do more than you ever thought possible. You wouldn't get your CDL to drive an SUV for instance and whipping out your driver's license isn't going to get you into the Pentagon. You need government clearance for that.

Understanding love and what kind of love you need is like that. You took the test for a romantic kind of love, but you're still hung up over the love you didn't get from family. Now you're sabotaging yourself, looking for the approval that you never got from a father figure in the arms of men who think it's sexy when you call them "daddy."

As you've probably learned by now, knowing is the first step to understanding. According to the ancient Greeks there are seven different types of love that a person will or can experience in their lifetime. I believe that finding fulfillment in each of these areas makes you better equipped to find and maintain the love you deserve.

The first type of love, the one that people are the most familiar with, is called Eros. This kind of love is all about sexuality and passion. According to myth, Eros is the madness that consumes those struck by Cupid's arrows. That blind, senseless, Romeo and Juliet type obsession that so many people view as the be-all and end-all of true romance.

The second type of love, Philia, is the love shared between friends. These relationships are built on shared interests and trust. Next to romantic love, it's the strongest kind of bond that you can share with another person outside of family. There are many instances where a couple will transition from this love to Eros. This can be mutual, or it can be one-sided, which is when the term "friend-zoned" most often comes into play. Coincidentally, Eros is made stronger when Philia is also a part of the mix. So many successful couples talk about how their partner is their best friend. Believe me, it isn't just a turn of phrase. While a romantic relationship can be successful without two people being friends first, it does help regarding longevity. After all, every relationship needs a stronger foundation than sex since the physical is fleeting and passions can cool.

Storge, the third kind of love, is familial love. This is the love that you find between parents and children, siblings, and so forth. This kind of love is forged from dependency and familiarity. Unlike other types of love, Storge is emotion established as a result of a relationship rather than the other way around. "Of course, I love her, she's my mother." These kinds of statements have nothing to do with the person themselves, but who the people are to one another. There are plenty of instances where families dislike one another on a personal level but still love each other for the roles they play in the family unit.

As I mentioned earlier, dysfunction in the relationships here can leave you searching for solace in your romantic interactions. If you've ever met a woman with "daddy issues" or dated a man who was a "momma's boy" then you understand what this looks like. Searching for your parents within the arms of your lovers goes much deeper than that though. Family is the first social dynamic that we're introduced to. We learn how to cope with our emotions by watching our parents and guardians. That's why abusive or addictive behavior is often passed down from one generation to the next. If one of your parents was addicted to drugs or alcohol, then the chances of you abusing substances as well to deal with stress or high emotion is much higher. If physical or verbal abuse was a normal part of your childhood, then when you grow up, you're more likely to search out that behavior in a romantic partner.

This is how cycles continue.

It's not just about recognizing the toxic behavior but understanding where it came from in the first place and how it's shaped your life up until this point. Given enough time, Storge is a by-product of Eros. Whether it's healthy or not depends on what habits you've carried over from your own family. While many of my clients are mothers already, there are just as many who aren't. So many of them are freezing their eggs, in a panic because they spend most of their time dating unavailable men and are afraid that they may never get the chance to conceive naturally and find a healthy version of Storge for themselves. Their biological clocks are ticking and these men, many of whom already have children of their own with former partners, make false promises that string them along and keep them hopeful for a love that they will never help assuage.

The next three types of love are rarely talked about. Agape—universal love—is the love you feel for your fellow man and the world around you. It is the love you experience through faith and it's the foundation that allows us to learn empathy and compassion. This is the kind of love that keeps us grounded and realistic. Through Agape, we learn not to give just one man complete control over our love or our capacity to love. When you don't believe or love something bigger than yourself, then you get into the habit of searching for God in mortal men. This leads to obsession, drug abuse, and codependency. Agape, when experienced in a healthy way, cultivates our potential as mates and hones our natural instincts of altruism. We want to give, to contribute to the greater good. The "greater good" can mean our community, the world at large, or our romantic relationship. Agape encourages us to contribute to what enriches us and leave it better than what it was when we found it.

Ludus is a playful love. Flirting, teasing, dancing, and playing; it's the kind of love that focuses on no-strings-attached affection. The kind that you find with Mr. Right Now. Ludus requires both parties to be on the same page emotionally. When they aren't, it's easy to confuse Ludus for Eros. In fact, most relationship issues today arise because of this exact problem. That's why communication is so important so that you can determine whether the man of your dreams is on the same page or if he's simply waiting around until you're smart enough to wake up.

Pragma is love based on practicality and duty. If you've ever been with someone because they "make sense" or check all your boxes, then you've experienced Pragma. It's possible to fall in love with who they are, but the passion of Eros and even the camaraderie of Philia is nowhere to be found.

Sound familiar?

The last kind of love, and the most important in my opinion, is Philautia.

Self-love.

Like the ones that came before it, self-love can exhibit itself in both healthy and unhealthy ways. The state of which can determine which form of love it transforms into or coexists with. If you don't love yourself, you're likely to have an unhealthy version of Eros, for example. We've discussed self-love multiple times during the course of this book, and for good reason. It really does dictate the direction of your love life and your ability to heal from trauma. It determines how we interact with ourselves, our family, our friends, lovers, and the world. Self-love is impossible without first knowing who you are, which brings us right back to the idea of the ID.

When you look at that photograph on the front, do you recognize the woman there? Would she recognize you if she were standing in front of you today? How have you changed and have the changes been for the better or worse? Self-love and self-reflection allow you to examine all the ways in which love has made itself known in your life. Through practice, you can determine where love has fallen short or blurred the lines between what was expected of it and what it became. Some relationships that I've been in were only meant to last for a season, yet I treated them as if they were my happily ever after. From dating someone who should have only ever been a friend, to remaining in abusive and unhealthy relationships because I had been taught to see toxicity as passion.

These were the kinds of mistakes that I made when I didn't know myself. I had lost my ID without ever realizing it and was desperately trying to remember the woman I had always seen myself as. Something that became increasingly hard to do each time that ID disappeared. For every failed relationship I was so busy going through those pesky stages of grief that I didn't realize until it was too late that I was missing something of true value.

ACTION STEP FOR SUCCESS: Accountability and Awareness

Method: Keep track of yourself. Know who you give yourself to—emotionally, physically, or mentally—and just how much you give away. Where are you and how much of you is left? What have you had to do, what price have you had to pay in order to get back to who you were? If that price is to high, it may be time to stop frequenting that establishment.

Exercise: Draw a picture of how you see yourself. It doesn't have to be accurate. This is more about determining how you see yourself than anything. From there divide the picture into several sections based on how much each kind of love defines you. For example, are you happier in your familial relationships or your romantic ones? Do you have more friendships than boyfriends? What versions of love are the most important to you? From there, assess the most significant relationships in your life and determine which category each falls into. Do they fulfill the version of love they represent for you or is something missing? How has that lack affected other versions of love? How do both affect your overall image of yourself? You can also perform this exercise with a bucket and some colored balls, pieces of paper, or etc. Each color will represent a certain type of love. When you fill the bucket with the relationships in your life, which colors are missing or overpowered by the others? Once you have an idea of where you stand overall, remove a colored item that represents an unhealthy relationship from each of the categories. What are you left with? This exercise is meant to give you a visual representation of exactly how much of your identity is tied up into relationships that aren't working. How does what you see make you feel at the end of the day and what can you do to improve the image before you? Write out a game plan and then stick to it.

Chapter 11: *Perfume*
A SYMPHONY OF INGREDIENTS

> *We accept the love we think we deserve.*
> *—Stephen Chbosky,*
> *The Perks of Being a Wallflower*

A woman's choice of perfume has always been the silent way she expresses herself to the world. I know people whose first and strongest memories of the women in their lives revolved around the scent of their perfume. For women, it's a rite of passage to find just the right scent: the one that defines who you are and how you feel.

Are you sensual?

Studious?

Understated with a hint of Japanese cherry blossom?

I've been one of each at various points in my life. Sometimes I'm all of those things at once or none of them at all. It's my prerogative to be as multifaceted as the perfumes I choose to adorn my skin. When I can, I like to keep a travel-sized version of my larger bottle in my purse for emergencies. It's a simple way to fortify my defenses throughout the day, a simple way to remind myself of the who I wanted to be when I stepped out of my house that morning. Because that's what perfume is: an identity that isn't always our own but rather one we've laid claim to. Like the moon and the seasons, our choice of perfume is often subject to change depending on how we feel, where we are in our lives, and what we're doing at a given moment. The perfume I wear to work is different than what I wear around my man or out for a night on the town.

Perfume has learned to be many things all at once: a combination of ingredients and smells that somehow comes together in perfect harmony. Much like perfume, relationships require a symphony of ingredients and timing in order to thrive. When I was younger, I gravitated towards scents that would make me feel like a woman. But once I got my hands on them, I realized that they didn't suit me. I was still growing, still changing, my body chemistry and hormones still in the process of maturing. In those days I was "young, dumb, and full of cum," as my auntie would say. So eager to grow up that I was sure I knew everything, including what I wanted in a man.

When I was older, those same perfumes that seemed too overpowering when I was young made more sense. Now, they fit. From time to time I still go through moments where a scent I once loved no longer seems to appeal to me the same way. Sometimes my love for a perfume will come back years later, and sometimes it won't because my preferences are different.

Your tastes can change. The way that you want to present yourself to the world can change. What you need from one relationship to the next can shift just as easily. What you may have wanted in a man during one season of your life may no longer fulfill you in the same way later. The trick is to know what appeals to you. While the overall smell of my favorite perfumes may be different now, I still gravitate towards certain notes. Some women are drawn to vanilla or rich, earthy smells like sandalwood. What attracts you? Find your core because that tells you what may draw your interest in the future.

The same is true for finding a significant other. Remember, how you present yourself to the world is what you attract and vice versa. Putting on certain perfumes can attract different people into your lives. When you understand what you want, you understand what you need to do to get it. Including the perfume, or collection of ingredients, that will bring you the love you deserve. Perfume highlights the need for inner harmony more so than any of the other items in your purse because it requires balance. Too much and you risk driving people away. Too little and it may not be enough to attract what you're looking for.

Those who are already in a relationship owe it to themselves and their partners to determine whether they're a good fit. If things have been rocky between you and your significant other, besides going to couple's counseling, there are exercises that the two of you can do together to determine where the disconnect lies.

Compatibility Quiz

---

1. Are you an introvert or an extrovert? What about your partner?

    _____

    _____

    _____

    _____

2. What is your communication speed?

    _____

    _____

    _____

    _____

3. What is your partner's communication speed?

    _____

    _____

    _____

    _____

4. What is your love language? How does it differ from your significant other's? How is it similar?

    _____

    _____

    _____

    _____

5. What are your interests?

    _____

    _____

    _____

    _____

6. What is your activity level both as a couple and individually?

_____

_____

_____

_____

7. How would you describe the tone of your relationship? Bored? Laid back? Enthusiastic? Chaotic?

_____

_____

_____

_____

8. How would you describe your sexual appetite?

_____

_____

_____

_____

9. Are you a learner or a know-it-all? What about your partner?

_____

_____

_____

_____

10. What are your goals for your relationship? Where do you see things going a year from now? How about five?

_____

_____

_____

_____

11. What is your commitment level to your partner?

_____

_____

_____

_____

12. What are you the most insecure about?

_____

_____

_____

_____

13. How do you cope with jealousy and misunderstandings?

_____

_____

_____

_____

14. How do you reconcile after arguments?

_____

_____

_____

_____

15. Who is the alpha in the relationship? If you both consider your-
    selves to be the alpha, what sort of problems has this created in
    your dynamic and who is responsible for fulfilling "beta" roles?

_____

_____

_____

_____

16. Do you choose obligations over what you love? Does he? What are these obligations and what makes them so important? Do you share similar ones, or can you understand why your partner made the choice that he/she did?

_____

_____

_____

_____

You and your partner should take the time to answer these questions first separately and then together. It can be enlightening to get a glimpse of how one of you views the other. In many cases conflicts arise because of miscommunication. You don't hear or see your partner for who they truly are or for what they can bring to the table so when you analyze the part they play in your relationship you're seeing them through a broken lens. This quiz is designed to get that communication ball rolling and determine exactly what kind of scent each of you is wearing for the other. If something doesn't smell right, it might be time to switch out a few of your ingredients, or ditch that scent altogether.

ACTION STEPS FOR SUCCESS: Self-Love and Honesty

Method: Set the standard so that any man who comes into your life knows from the start what you expect. If you're already in a relationship, take the time to listen to your partner. To truly see them. What are their ingredients? Are you fulfilling them in the same way that you expect to be fulfilled? If not, then what can you do to fix things?

Exercise: You've read dozens of affirmations, so write a few of your own. Cater to each of your ingredients as if you were an expensive brand of perfume. Are you an orange zest—tangy and vibrant with a little bite? Or do you think of yourself as more of a vanilla kind of woman—sweet, savory, and in need of a little coddling in order to appreciate your more subtle notes. This is a fun exercise to play with a partner. What ingredients would they use to describe you and your lovemaking, for instance. Don't be afraid to have some fun with it. Oftentimes, communicating is much easier to do when the atmosphere is light and nonjudgmental.

Chapter 12: *Phone Charger*

A SOURCE OF POWER

> *There was a time in the marriage when I could no longer look at myself in a mirror, couldn't feel I was a nice person. A bad relationship can do that, can make you doubt everything good you ever felt about yourself.*
> *—Dionne Warwick*

Never underestimate the importance of keeping an extra charger handy. I can't tell you how many times I've realized halfway through a trip that my battery was running low. These days, a person does everything through his or her phone. They communicate with loved ones, they take and store photos in an ever-growing gallery of memories, they answer work emails and keep up with obligations through calendar events and pre-set reminders. Our phones help us discover new information, entertain us during moments of boredom, and even light the way when the world has gone too dark too see by. For billions of people, their phone is their lifeline, their connection to the source, and when that battery gets low…

Well, there's no telling what happens then.

Now, when I say "connection to the source" I mean a couple of different things. This is your connection to other people as well as your connection to your spirituality and morals. The "source" is whatever keeps you grounded and true to yourself, and therefore it can take many different forms. Cell phones are such an ingrained part of our lives, and therefore our relationships, that it's impossible to comprehend how many couples have come together and drifted apart because of a call, a photo, or a text. While I hold to the belief that texting is no way to communicate, our phones play other equally tangible roles in our relationships. When you depend on something that much, you're bound to share a few similarities, and there are two things that people, and cell phones have in common:

-    They both come in various colors and sizes.

-    They both need recharging on a regular basis.

Think of every relationship in your life from work to family as an app. Some are simple

and use up little energy. Some apps run in the background, never making themselves known until the moment they're needed. Then there are the battery drainers. You know the ones. In fact, you could probably name several off the top of your head right this second. A relationship is defined as: *"the relation connecting or binding participants in a relationship: such as a specific instance or type of kinship, a state of affairs existing between those having relations or dealings, or a romantic or passionate attachment."*

Like "trauma," "relationship" is also a noun. And, like trauma, a bad relationship can drain you. It doesn't care what you have going on or whether an outlet is nearby. When you're used to running on empty, you have to give up all those other things you found joy in for fear that even the simplest of them will use up what little reserves you have left. We know that our personal traumas play a major role in the relationships we gravitate towards. Domestic violence, drug and alcohol abuse, PTSD, post-slavery stress disorder (PSSD), sexual assault, the loss of a loved one, breakups, divorce, physical trauma, STDs and STIs are all events that happen in our lives that can affect our ability to establish healthy relationships. With so much weighing us down, it can be next to impossible to recognize the signs of a partner who is leaving you emotionally drained.

In the grand scheme of things, an uneven give-and-take may not seem like much, but it can be more devastating in the long run than you think. A healthy relationship not only inspires but energizes you. It accepts what you have to offer without taking from you. There's a huge difference between accepting something that is being given freely and taking: the main component of which is trust. Trust is a necessary foundation in any relationship and without it, it's all too easy to violate that trust by demanding more from a partner than they're willing—or able—to give.

When you're with a partner who knows you and respects your limitations, there never comes a point where you feel as if you're being drained. They don't push past your boundaries and demand that you give and give all in the name of "love." A mature partner who brings something to the table will give as much as he receives. He will be your port in the storm, your extra charger in the middle of nowhere when that little bar on your screen flashes from yellow to red. The person you love should be your peace. If your relationship doesn't provide that for you, then you'll always be limited in how far you can go both individually and as a couple because you'll constantly be stuck near the closest outlet, desperately trying to recharge before your battery gets to low and your screen goes dark.

ACTION STEPS FOR SUCCESS: Self-Care

Method: When it comes to loving yourself and attracting healthy relationships, self-care is paramount. Get used to pampering yourself, to being kind to yourself. No man with bad intentions will be able to dazzle you if you know what it takes to romance yo' damn self. This is a great way to recharge in between relationships as well as during them. Whether your partner leaves you feeling energized or not, it's important not to rely on someone else to keep your battery fully charged. That would be unfair to the both of you.

Exercise: This is the time to play checks and balances. Write out what your partner does for you emotionally and vice versa. If you're the only one giving—or receiving—then how does that imbalance affect your relationship? Like communication, it's important to reciprocate. Be a source of power as well and remember that it's OK to need someone to lean on every now and again so long as you don't forget how to stand on your own two feet.

Chapter 13: *Final Thoughts*

It's said that all is fair in love and war, but I know for a fact that love shouldn't look like a battlefield. Riddled with hurts, both new and old, and reeking of lost hope. Love shouldn't be something you have to heal from. It shouldn't be yet another synonym that we use for "trauma."

Throughout my career I've seen hundreds of relationships where couples fight like cats and dogs. Something in the equation, their communication, their love language, the use of boundaries, etc., doesn't work. Yet many women are all too willing to cling to the toxic if only because it's familiar. That familiarity has taught them that they'll never have anything better. That "communicating" meant stepping into the ring with the world's heavyweight boxing champion.

A relationship should not be the place you go to get torn down, leaving you scarred beyond recognition and scorned by the part of you that still believes in values you abandoned for the sake of companionship. This process of hurting one another, particularly in black relationships, comes from the lingering trauma of slavery. Black lovers were routinely ripped apart and the stronger the bond between them the more likely that love would be used against them. Recent studies have proven that if an experience is traumatic enough, it etches itself in our DNA and passes itself down to our children. It's the same evolutionary technique that gives us an instinctive fear of things that would have haunted the cavemen, like snakes or spiders.

Trauma can be such an encompassing and devastating event that it can linger for generation after generation. Unless, of course, we learn to heal from it. Learn to unshackle the ghost of those chains that were unlocked so long ago but still weigh so many of us down. Everyone has the ability to let go of the dysfunctionality that exists in their lives, to undo the patterns that shaped every toxic relationship they found themselves in. Healing can take a lot of different forms and the path to a healthy and fulfilling relationship can be long and winding. Just remember that there are tools that you can use to turn it all around.

Content	Lesson
1. Mirror	Hold on to your values
2. Sewing Kit	Faith and spirituality are the glue that holds it all together
3. Keys	Affirmations can be your secret weapon
4. Panty Liners	Avoiding the issue never solved anything
5. Pepper Spray	Set boundaries or risk repeating the same mistakes repeatedly
6. Tissue	Mourn the loss and keep it moving
7. Lip Gloss	Communication is key for a healthy relationship
8. ID	Keep track of who you are and what you want out of a relationship

9. Perfume	Attract what you need and not just what you want
10. Phone Charger	Love should leave you rejuvenated rather than drained

For those who feel that they can't do it alone or who aren't sure where to start, there are always trained professionals like myself to help you work through it all. In the interim, if you've read this far, I want to thank you for going on this journey with me. I pray that with the skills you've developed over the course of this book that finding your own happily ever after will be just a little bit easier.

With Affinity & Harmony,

Montrella Cowan, MSW, LICSW, a.k.a "Shernetter"

~ A relationship should NOT tear you down! Check your purse contents. ~

Chapter 14: *Conclusion*

Shaking your head, you pull your phone from the charger with a sigh and stuff both back in your purse. The sound of the zipper gliding closed is like a round of applause for a job well done. You're finally through; your purse is lighter without so much weighing it down and you smile, feeling good. It's been several long minutes since you decided to clean out all the junk and you gather up the trash on the coffee table and head into the kitchen to toss it. The doorbell rings and you hurry back towards your purse, swinging the strap over your shoulder. A solitary Band-Aid, still in its wrapper, catches your attention and you hesitate. For a moment you contemplate throwing it away, but then think better of it.

What if you get hurt tonight?

What if you fall?

These shoes are as new as the purse once was and you may slip in them, may fumble. It would be embarrassing but it's nothing that hasn't happened before. You're a big girl and by now you know how to get up when life has knocked you down. You also know that it doesn't hurt to have something to patch up the scrapes and bruises until the safety of home lets you lick them clean again. Without a second thought, you slip the Band-Aid in next to all of the other items you've decided to keep and hurry towards the door. You aren't afraid of getting hurt, but you've learned to always be prepared. Besides, you're sure your date will appreciate a woman who thinks ahead, especially if he happens to be the one who needs a little TLC before the night is through.

About the Author

Montrella Cowan, MSW, LICSW is the founder and CEO of Affinity Health Affairs, LLC, a private psychotherapy practice. Montrella is a personal trauma and relationship expert. As a licensed independent clinical social worker, she is trusted for her high-quality service, wisdom-from-experience, personal care, and passion to help women, men, and teens to have healthy relationships with themselves, their partners, and their families. In addition to her private practice in Washington, DC, Montrella's "practical approach" niche has helped her to become a widely sought-after motivational speaker and trainer on national and international platforms. She has been featured on Essence Magazine, Radio One, and other media outlets.

Montrella earned a bachelor's degree in Interdisciplinary Studies and Social Work from Catholic University and a master's degree in Social Work from Howard University. Montrella is from Brooklyn, NY, but currently resides in Washington, DC. She is a proud mother of two children. Among many associations, Montrella is most honored to be a member of the First Baptist Church of Glenarden in Prince George's County, Maryland, the National Association of Black Social Workers, and Delta Sigma Theta Sorority.

Let's Stay Connected!

Web: https://affinity411.com/
Online courses: https://MontrellaCowan.com
Instagram: https://www.instagram.com/affinity411/
Twitter: https://twitter.com/Affinity411
Facebook: https://www.facebook.com/maffinity411/
Email: Help@MyLuvLife.com or Montrella@Affinity411.com

About the Publisher

At **the Vision to Fruition Publishing House,** we are dedicated to helping others bring their personal, business, ministry, and other visions to fruition. Whether it's as grand as a book you want to write, a business you want to start, a conference or event you want to host, a ministry you want to launch or an organization you want to start; or as small as needing a computer repair, logo design or web design; **The Vision to Fruition Publishing House** is the publishing branch of **the Vision to Fruition Group.** We will help you walk through the process and set you up for success!

At **the Vision to Fruition Group** we don't have clients, we have *Visionaries.* We provide solutions to equip others to pursue their visions and dreams with reckless abandon. Since 2017, we have published over 30 authors, several of which were Amazon Bestsellers. We would love for you to join our family of Visionaries as well!

Learn more here: **www.vision-fruition.com**